Heartfelt

Heartfelt

25 projects for stitched and felted accessories

teresa searle

🦁 **ST. MARTIN'S GRIFFIN**

NEW YORK

Ⓜ

SILVER BAY PUBLIC LIBRARY

HEARTFELT. Copyright © 2006 by
Breslich & Foss Ltd.
All rights reserved. Printed in China.
No part of this book may be used or
reproduced in any manner whatsoever
without written permission except in the
case of brief quotations embodied in
critical articles or reviews. For
information, address St. Martin's Press,
175 Fifth Avenue, New York, N.Y. 10010.

www.stmartins.com

Text by **Teresa Searle**
Photographs by **Shona Wood**

Library of Congress Cataloging-in-
Publication Data Available Upon Request

ISBN-10: 0-312-36214-5
ISBN-13: 978-0-312-36214-0

First U.S. Edition: November 2006

10 9 8 7 6 5 4 3 2 1

contents

Introduction 6

Techniques 8

THE PROJECTS 20

Midnight Flower Hat 22

Russian Hat 28

Star and Button Purse 32

Glasses Case 36

Lavender Needle Case 40

Starburst Handbag 44

Tote Bag 50

Flower Mittens 54

Oriental Slippers 58

Ipod Case 62

Sapphire Scarf 66

Freeform Scarf 68

Rose Accessories 70

Daisy Barrette 74

Pom-pom Hair Band 76

Love-heart Pin 78

Bubble Scarf and Bag 82

CHILDREN'S PROJECTS

Earflap Hat 86

Children's Mittens 90

Butterfly Baby Coat 94

Cosmic Baby Blanket 100

Heartwarming Scarf 104

Bunny Slippers 108

Backpack With Bird 112

Patterns 116

Suppliers and Credits 127

Index 128

introduction

FELTED KNITTING HAS A LONG HISTORY. FELT HAS BEEN USED FOR HAT MAKING FOR CENTURIES, AND IN RECENT YEARS, FELTED KNITTING HAS BECOME extremely fashionable with many clothes and textile designers exploring the possibilities of this material to make garments, hats, and all kinds of accessories.

Felted knitting has a great deal in common with other felting processes, involving the application of heat, moisture, and friction to cause the wool fibers to bind together to create a felted fabric. However, instead of making the felt directly from raw materials, in this case you create a knitted fabric from yarn before applying the felting process. This produces a fabric that has the texture and appearance of felt but the flexibility of knitting.

Felted knitting is comfortable to wear. Its felted structure also means that it can be cut without fraying, making it ideal for appliqué and embroidery projects. As well as using yarn to create new pieces of felted knitting, you can also recycle existing pieces of knitting by making use of interesting finds in thrift stores or that favorite sweater that has accidentally shrunk in the wash.

This book features a wide range of accessories, and explores a range of hand and machine processes to suit all abilities and access to equipment. The book is intended to be both instructional and inspirational. Do not feel that you have to copy the projects rigidly— adapt them with some of your own ideas and color schemes. Many of the motifs can be transferred to other projects, and there are some handy tips on page 15 to encourage you to try producing your own unique designs.

teresa searle

Techniques

In this section, you will find all the information you need to recreate the accessories in the book and to develop your own designs. After a section on choosing appropriate yarns and creating felted machine and hand knitting, there is an illustrated guide to the embroidery stitches used in the projects. Refer to these when following the project instructions, but feel free to experiment and create your own motifs.

materials and equipment

As well as the main fabric used to make the projects—felted knitting—you will also need hand and machine embroidery threads as well as a variety of other embellishments, such as buttons and beads. If you plan to make only the smaller projects, basic sewing and knitting equipment will suffice. If you intend to make larger projects or produce quite a bit of work using felted knitting, you will find a sewing machine and perhaps a knitting machine very useful.

In the sewing basket

- ♥ Needles: *sewing and embroidery*
- ♥ Pins: *flat flower pins or glass-headed dressmaking pins are best*
- ♥ Knitting needles: *to hand knit felt for small projects.*
- ♥ Thimble: *useful when hand sewing through several thick layers of felt*
- ♥ Scissors: *paper, embroidery and large fabric scissors*
- ♥ Rotary cutter and mat: *to cut out multiple shapes and patterns*
- ♥ Threads: *many can be used by hand or machine. Polyester sewing threads; rayon machine embroidery threads; wool machine embroidery threads; hand embroidery threads.*

Hardware

- ♥ Sewing machine: *to make up projects and embellish them with embroidery*
- ♥ Serger: *to trim, stitch, overcast, and add decorative finishes. While not essential, it is useful for making up hats and jackets.*
- ♥ Knitting machine: *to make large amounts of felted knitting*
- ♥ Washing machine: *essential whether you are felting machine or hand knitting. Felting by hand is very hard work!*

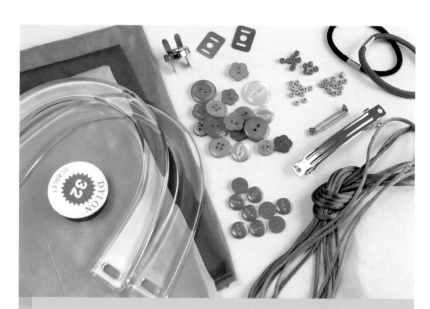

To add a professional finish to your work, pay attention to fastenings and other details. Dyable plastic handles and colorful cord are useful. Buttons can be gleaned from thrift stores and asian fabric suppliers are a good source of silk for linings.

felted knitting

FELTED KNITTING CAN BE MADE BY HAND OR MACHINE, OR BY FELTING KNITWEAR SOURCED FROM FRIENDS, RELATIVES, OR THRIFT STORES. FELTED KNITTING IS CERTAINLY AN ART RATHER THAN A SCIENCE. IT IS IMPOSSIBLE TO SAY HOW MUCH A YARN OR PIECE OF KNITWEAR WILL FELT UNLESS YOU TRY IT OUT FOR YOURSELF. AS YOU VENTURE INTO THIS CRAFT, YOU WILL GRADUALLY BECOME MORE CONFIDENT WITH CHOOSING THE RIGHT FIBERS AND JUDGING FOR YOURSELF HOW SUCCESSFUL THEY ARE LIKELY TO BE.

suitable yarns

It is important to choose the right type of yarn—yarns made from pure synthetic or plant fibers will not felt, for example. Choose a yarn that is 100 percent wool or has a high wool content. Some fiber blends, such as lambswool and nylon, will still felt effectively. Make sure that the yarn is not a superwash wool that has been treated to be machine washable. Other factors, such as dyeing and bleaching during industrial processing, will also greatly influence a yarn's ability to felt.

Shetland wool comes in a lovely range of colors, felts very easily, and is reasonably priced. It can, however, be scratchy to wear, so if you prefer a softer felt or are making items for babies, lambswool is a better option. Lambswool felts more readily than Shetland wool, also comes in beautiful colors, but is more expensive to buy. Other types of wool fibers also felt well, and you will get different results depending on the type of wool and breed of sheep. You'll find a list of suppliers of suitable yarns on page 127.

test samples

Before investing a large amount of money on yarn, make test samples to check that your chosen yarn will felt, how much it will shrink, and at what temperature you get the best results. Keep notes so you can replicate the successful tests with the real piece of knitting.

Work samples of 50 stitches by 50 rows. Measure the sample then follow the felting process (see page 14). Measure it after felting to assess how much it has shrunk.

Knitted fabric can shrink substantially during the felting process, so you will probably need a piece of knitting 50-100 percent larger than the piece of felt required. You may find it has shrunk more lengthwise that widthwise, so allow for this when knitting up pieces for your projects. Knitting may curl at the edges and felt to itself, particularly if using stockinette stitch on a knitting machine. This will make the edge of the knitting unusable for the main pieces of the project, so allow for this when deciding how large a piece to knit. The rolled edge does have its charms, however, and can be cut off as a strip and be used for cords and ties.

machine knitting

Having access to a knitting machine will enable you to make large pieces of felted knitting with much less effort than hand knitting. It will give you creative freedom to experiment with the knitting as well as ambition in the size of work you are making. If you machine knit 2 lb. (1 kg) of yarn in one go, you will get several yards or meters of fabric to use in one large project or several smaller ones.

Use a fine 2-ply fingering-weight machine knitting yarn. It should be between 2/8 and 2/11—this refers to the manufacturer's system of measuring the thickness of yarn. Consult your manual for basics, such as threading the machine. Cast on with the yarn and knit up rectangles of the colors you would like to use. Remember that your felt will shrink considerably: how many stitches and rows you work should reflect this.

Using a loose gauge is important because the wool fibers need space to move around before interlocking together. Set your machine gauge to 10 and adjust later tests if necessary. Stockinette stitch will create felt with a smooth texture, but you can experiment with other stitches to create felt of different textures.

Do not worry about binding off properly because the felting process makes this unnecessary. Simply take the knitting off the machine and proceed to the felting process described on page 14.

MACHINE KNITTING A SCARF

Several projects in this book involve embellishing a scarf made from a length of felted knitting. Follow these instructions to make a scarf about 60 x 12 in. (150 x 30 cm) after felting. Cast on 70 stitches and knit in stockinette stitch for 750 rows using a loose gauge, such as 10. Vary the colors as you wish. Remove the knitting from the machine or bind off following the instructions in the manual, then felt the piece. You will probably find that the edges have rolled in and felted together, forming a firm edge. If you want to eliminate this, carefully work down the curl with a sharp craft knife, uncurling as you go. Press firmly with a steam iron and pressing cloth, then decorate.

The felting process transforms both the appearance and properties of machine knitting

hand knitting

Hand knitting yarn for felting is feasible for small projects such as corsages, purses, and small bags. It can, however, be disheartening to see a piece of knitting that has taken a long time to knit shrink to up to half its original size. Use 4-ply sport-weight (2/4) hand knitting yarn that is suitable for felting, or knit with a double strand of machine knitting yarn. The end result will be thicker than machine knitted yarn, but is still usable for many items.

The knitting needs to be looser than normal so the wool fibers have room to move around before matting together, so use knitting needles that are two sizes bigger than those recommended on the ball band. As with machine knitting, you can experiment with various hand stitches to produce different felt textures if you wish.

Felt is a lovely material from which to make entire garments or smaller accessories, like this rose

Hand knitting yarn for felting is feasible for small projects such as corsages, purses, and small bags.

USING RECYCLED SWEATERS

Making felted knitting is a hit and miss affair, especially when it comes to recycling. You may find that a sweater will not felt however many times you wash it. You may also find that some sweaters felt too thick to be usable. These tips will help you source knitwear that will be successful.

♥ *Look at the label to determine the fiber content. Pure lambswool, Shetland wool, merino, mohair, and cashmere are best. Knitwear that has wool mixed with a synthetic fiber such as nylon may also be successful. If the knitwear has no animal fiber content, it will not felt.*

♥ *If the label says "handwash only," it is likely the sweater will felt successfully. Machine-washable knitwear and yarns are to be avoided because they have been specially treated not to shrink or felt.*

the felting process

Felting depends on three factors—heat, moisture, and friction. Large amounts of knitting provide their own friction, so if you are felting 2 lb. (1 kg) of knitting at a time, this will provide sufficient friction. If you are felting a small amount, place jeans or flip-flops into the machine to add friction. Choose items that will not shed lint, which will stick to the felt and may even become part of it.

Sort your knitwear into color groups, because once in the washing machine, fibers from one color may transfer onto others. Washing detergent changes the Ph factor of the wool and contributes to the felting process. Most detergents intended for colored fabrics are suitable for felting. Add the dose recommended on the box.

Gauging the correct temperature is vital. Too cold and felting may not occur; too hot and you may end up with felt that is far too thick to use. As a general guide, the following temperatures apply: 140°F (60°C) for Shetland wool and 90°F (30°C) for lambswool. Choose a cycle that lasts about 1^1/$_2$ hours, including rinsing and spinning. If you have a top-loading machine, open the machine at regular intervals to check how the felting is progressing. Your felted knitting is ready when it is difficult to see the individual stitches.

CARING FOR FELTED KNITTING

DRYING: *The easiest way to dry newly felted knitting is to put it in a tumble dryer, which will also soften and fluff the felt. Tumble drying will felt the fabric a little further.*

CLEANING: *Dry-cleaning is the best method; hand washing is a good second. Machine washing will make felt items shrink further, so handwash them with a gentle soap and lukewarm water, rubbing very gently. When drying a hat or slippers, place lightly rolled tissue inside to hold their shape. Light soiling can be brushed off; tougher stains may require dry cleaning.*

PRESSING: *Roll out any seams with your fingertips, then place a cotton cloth onto the surface of the fabric to protect the embroidery. Use a steam iron set on a high temperature to press the surface, avoiding rubbing movements that may distort the knitting. You may find a sleeve board useful when pressing awkward shapes, such as hats. Manipulate the felted knitting back into shape while it is still warm and damp.*

With experience and a little experimentation, you can develop your own style and design ideas

design tips

ONCE YOU ARE CONFIDENT WITH USING FELTED KNITTING, YOU WILL WANT TO ADAPT THE IDEAS IN THIS BOOK OR DESIGN YOUR OWN PROJECTS. HERE ARE SOME IDEAS ON GAINING INSPIRATION FOR YOUR WORK AS WELL AS SOME PRACTICAL TIPS FOR WORKING WITH APPLIQUÉ AND USING COLOR.

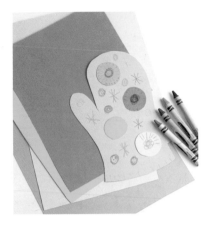

EXPERIMENT WITH COLLAGE

A really good way to develop appliqué designs is to use collage. Cut out the shape of your garment in a background color from paper or cardstock and then play around with other shapes, building up a layered design. Once you are happy with the design, stick the shapes in place and add detail using colored pencils or crayons. Try to keep shapes as large and simple as possible because small shapes are difficult to apply on and can fall apart.

KEEP A SCRAPBOOK

Make a scrapbook to keep cuttings, postcards, and photographs that will spark your imagination. You may find inspiration in architecture, mosaics, or folk art. Visit parks and gardens where you can take photos or make sketches. Look at the natural world; birds and animals may bring an idea to mind.

Once you have collected lots of visual information, start to design. Try out lots of ideas using a medium you feel confident with. You could draw them using colored pencils, crayons, or pastels, for example. The drawings shown below were done in oil pastels to form a resist, then watercolor was applied over the top.

CHOOSING COLORS

When deciding which colors to use, keep in mind that cool colors such as greens and blues recede, making them suitable for backgrounds, while warmer colors such as reds and pinks stand out, lending themselves more to motifs.

machine appliqué and embroidery

MACHINE EMBROIDERY LOOKS QUITE DIFFERENT FROM HAND STITCHING, BECAUSE THE MACHINED MOTIFS BECOME FULLY INTEGRATED WITH THE BACKGROUND FABRIC. YOU DO NOT NEED A SOPHISTICATED MACHINE TO ACHIEVE GOOD RESULTS, AND VERY SIMPLE STITCHES CAN BE USED TO ADD DETAIL TO MOTIFS. PRACTICE ON SCRAP PIECES OF FELT BEFORE YOU STITCH THE REAL ITEM. THE MORE YOU STITCH ONTO A PIECE OF FELT, THE MORE IT WILL STRETCH, SO ALLOW FOR THIS WHEN CUTTING PATTERNS FOR HATS AND GARMENTS.

APPLIQUÉ USING ZIGZAG STITCH

Appliqué is the process of stitching down pieces of fabric onto a background to form a pattern or design. Start by cutting out the motifs and pinning them onto the background fabric. Thread the machine with polyester sewing threads, which will not show up as much as thicker cotton threads. Set the machine to straight stitch and attach the presser foot, which is suitable for general stitching. Place the fabric under the presser foot, lining up the inside edge of the foot with the edge of the motif. Start with a few straight stitches to prevent the stitching from coming undone. Select zigzag stitch, choosing the longest and widest stitch setting because this will make stitching thick fabrics easier. Stitch around the edge of the motif, keeping the edge aligned with the inside edge of the presser foot. Finish with a few straight stitches.

MACHINE EMBROIDERY THREADS

Machine embroidery threads can be woolen, cotton, or metallic, and all of them are great fun to experiment with. Rayon embroidery threads have a wonderful shine that contrasts beautifully with the matte texture of felt. They are easy to use as the top thread on the sewing machine.

Some machine embroidery threads are a little thicker than normal, but they can be used more successfully on the bobbin. In this case, you will need to work with the wrong side of the fabric uppermost, and regularly turn it over to assess how the design is developing. Some finer hand embroidery threads can also be used in this way. Less tension is put on the thread and it does not need to be fed through a needle, both of which may cause the thread to break.

You may need to adjust the tension screw on the bobbin case by turning the screw a little at a time.

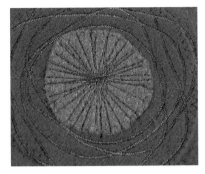

STRAIGHT STITCH

Straight stitch can be used to great effect to add detail to motifs such as leaves, birds' wings, and so on. Thread the machine with embroidery thread and select a long stitch, so that the thread floats over the surface rather than getting buried in the felt. Using the reverse function and stitching backward is easier than turning the work around.

TO STITCH LEAF VEINS

Start at the bottom of the leaf and sew up the center. Using the reverse lever, sew back down the center. Stitch forward for about $1/2$ in. (1 cm) then carry on to the outside of the leaf. Reverse back to the center. Continue in this way until you have stitched veins on one side of the leaf. Reverse back to the bottom and stitch veins going up the other side.

TO STITCH A STAR

Stitch a line forward for about 1 in. (2.5 cm), then reverse back to the beginning. Sew forward to the middle of the line, turn the fabric to the right by a few degrees, and continue the line. Reverse back to the beginning and stitch forward again, turning the fabric a few degrees to the right upon reaching the center. Repeat stitching and turning in this way to create a star.

SATIN STITCH

Satin stitch is made by adjusting the stitch length to its shortest. Choose how wide you would like it to be according to the design. On some machines it is possible to change its width while you are stitching, enabling you to taper the ends of lines. Start and finish satin stitch with a few straight stitches to help fasten off the ends and prevent unraveling. Use satin stitch to outline shapes and add broader lines to flowers, a bird's tail, and so on. If used in short bursts, it creates small dots that look like beads.

SET EMBROIDERY STITCHES

Set embroidery stitches can look rigid, but when mixed with other more random stitches, they can take on a new and less formulaic appearance. Consult your manual to explore the range of stitches available on your machine.

FREE-MOTION EMBROIDERY

Some sewing machines have a facility for lowering the feed dog so that you can move the fabric in any direction. Free-motion embroidery is the nearest thing to drawing with stitch, and is particularly useful when stitching circular shapes. It can also be used to manipulate felted knitting into three-dimensional textures. Although it is usually best to fit the fabric into an embroidery hoop for free-motion embroidery, this is unnecessary with felted knitting as well as difficult because the fabric is thick. You may need to buy a special presser foot if you do not have one.

hand appliqué and embroidery

HAND STITCHING LENDS A NAIVE HOMESPUN LOOK TO PROJECTS. IF USING SIX-STRANDED EMBROIDERY THREADS, DIVIDE THE STRANDS AND WORK WITH TWO STRANDS AT A TIME. YOU CAN ALSO USE THICK MACHINE EMBROIDERY THREADS FOR HAND EMBROIDERY, AGAIN USING TWO STRANDS AT A TIME. WITH OTHER THREADS, EXPERIMENT TO DISCOVER HOW MANY STRANDS ARE BEST TO WORK WITH.

BUTTONHOLE STITCH

Buttonhole stitch is firm and durable, and is used for both appliqué and decorative edgings. Working from left to right, insert the needle through a determined line. Loop the thread around the needle and bring the needle through the fabric, pulling the thread to form a stitch. Repeat the stitch at regular intervals along the edge. When you need to change thread, hide the remaining thread ends inside layers of fabric by taking them through with the needle.

STAB STITCH

This is simply taking the needle and thread through the fabric and back again to make a mark with the stitch. Here, it is being used to indicate the veins on a leaf.

RUNNING STITCH

This is one of the simplest of all hand embroidery stitches. Insert the needle in and out of the fabric at regular intervals, pulling the thread to form stitches as you go.

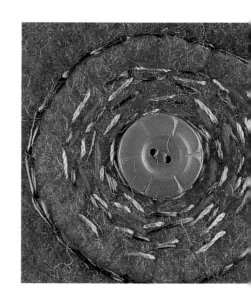

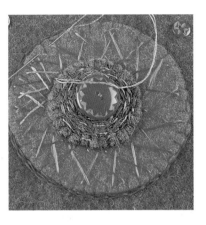

CROSS STITCH

Cross stitches can be scattered randomly on backgrounds or used to indicate features such as a rabbit's nose. Bring the thread up through the fabric and back down again to create a stitch. Bring the needle back up through the fabric at a parallel point and then back into the fabric, crossing over the existing stitch.

LAZY DAISY STITCH

This is very useful to indicate small flowers, either in backgrounds or over circles of felt. Insert the needle in and out of the fabric. Loop the thread around the needle and pull through. To hold the loop in position, insert the needle just below the point where it came up so that a small stitch is formed, tying down the previous thread.

HERRINGBONE STITCH

Here, two rows of this very decorative stitch have been worked one on top of the other. Determine two parallel lines. Take a small stitch from right to left on the upper line. Take the needle into the lower line a little to the right and take another stitch. Continue alternately on upper and lower lines.

BACK STITCH

This is effective if you want to make a solid line of stitching. Bring the needle and thread up through the fabric. Take a small stitch to the right, bringing the needle up again a little to the left of the original point. Continue in this way to make a line of stitching.

CHAIN STITCH

This is useful for making a prominent and decorative line of stitching around motifs. Insert the needle in and out of the fabric. Loop the thread around the needle and pull the needle and thread through to form a stitch. Insert the needle again where the thread last came up and repeat as above.

STAR STITCH

These are lovely to use in the center of flowers as well as dotted around the background. First, create a cross stitch as above. Then make another cross stitch over the top to form a star. To stabilize the stitch, make a much smaller cross stitch over the center of the star between the rays.

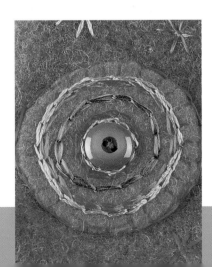

The Projects

On the following pages you will discover how to create a wide range of garments and accessories for both adults and children. Some of the pieces are more complex than others, but each of them is embellished with gorgeous appliqué and embroidery. Why not try your hand at a cozy hat or scarf that are perfect for a winter stroll, or make a pair of fun slippers or a colorful backpack for a child? You'll find pattern pieces and templates for the motifs in the templates section beginning on page 116.

midnight flower hat

THIS FUNKY FLORAL HAT IS EASY TO CONSTRUCT FROM RECTANGLES OF FELT. DECORATED WITH MACHINE APPLIQUÉ AND EMBROIDERY, BERRY-LIKE BEADS ADD THE PERFECT FINISHING TOUCH. MAKE THE HAT IN RICH SHADES OF RED AND PINK TO BRING A WARMING NOTE TO WINTERTIME WALKS.

MATERIALS

- ♥ 28 x 14 in. (70 x 35 cm) piece of dark red felted knitting
- ♥ small pieces of felted knitting or felt in shades of red and pink
- ♥ polyester sewing threads in matching colors
- ♥ rayon embroidery threads in matching colors
- ♥ about 70 small red beads

EQUIPMENT

- ♥ tape measure
- ♥ cardstock, pencil, ruler, and compass to make patterns and templates
- ♥ scissors—paper, fabric, and embroidery
- ♥ flat flower or glass-headed pins
- ♥ needles—sewing and beading
- ♥ sewing machine with free-motion embroidery function
- ♥ serger (optional)
- ♥ steam iron and pressing cloth

1 Measure the circumference of the head, then divide this figure in half and add $1/2$ in. (1 cm) for seam allowances. Draw a rectangle of this length and 8 in. (20 cm) high onto cardstock; this is the crown of the hat. Draw another rectangle $1/2$ in. (1 cm) shorter and 3 in. (7.5 cm) high; this is the cuff of the hat, which must be shorter to ensure a snug fit. Cut out the patterns. Fold the main piece of felt in half widthwise. Pin the patterns onto the felt so that the shorter edges align with the fold. Cut out the pieces.

2 When unfolded, you should have two long rectangles to form the crown and cuff of the hat. If you have made your own felt, cut off the rolled edges from the original piece and use these for the ties on top of the hat; you need one 23 in. (58 cm) and two 4 in. (10 cm) long ties. Otherwise, cut strips twice the desired width of cord, fold them in half lengthwise, and stitch along the edge to form the cords.

3 Make templates for the decoration. Use a compass to draw a 4 in. (10 cm) diameter circle for the round flower and a 2 in. (5 cm) diameter circle for the flower centers. Fold a 4 in. (10 cm) square of cardstock into quarters. Draw a spiky design across the folded square and cut out for the spiky flower.

This cozy hat is made in toning shades of one flattering color

4 Pin the templates onto the smaller pieces of felt. Cut out one spiky flower, two round flowers, and three flower centers in different shades.

5 Pin the flowers onto the crown of the hat, keeping the design toward the bottom edge and placing the spiky flower in the center. Using matching sewing thread, machine appliqué the flowers onto the hat using a large zigzag stitch.

4

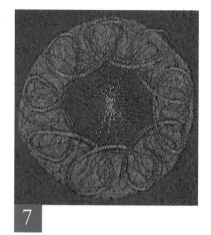

7

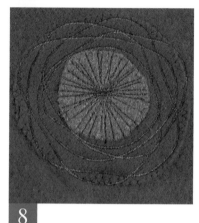

8

5

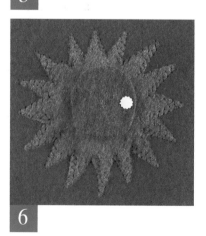

6

6 Pin and appliqué the centers of the flowers in place.

7 Using a wide satin stitch and rayon embroidery thread, embroider loops around the outer section of the left-hand round flower.

8 Using a narrow satin stitch, embroider overlapping wavy lines around the outer section of the right-hand round flower.

9

9 Using free-motion embroidery, embellish the outer section of the spiky flower with circles. Repeat on the inner section using a different color thread.

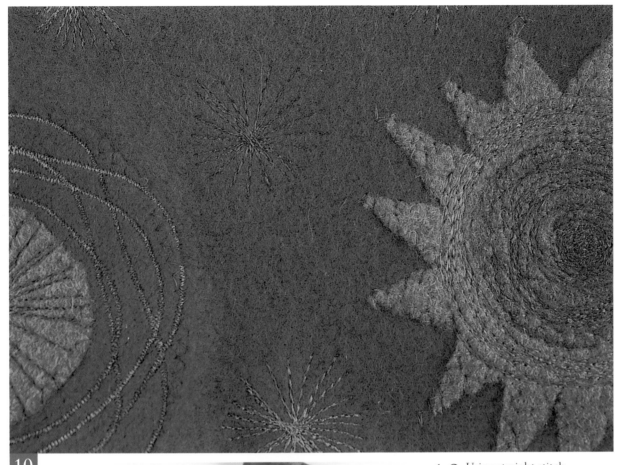

10

11

10 Using straight stitch, embroider the center of each round flower with a star. Use different color threads to stitch stars on the background surrounding each flower. Gently press the hat.

11 Sew small red beads around the outer sections of the round flowers and in the inner section of the spiky flower using matching sewing thread.

MAKING UP

12 Select a stretch stitch such as double overlock or zigzag, or use serger, to sew the hat pieces together. Fold the crown of the hat widthwise, right sides together, and sew the seam using a ¼ in. (5 mm) seam allowance and matching sewing thread. Refold the hat so that the seam is at the center back.

12

13

14

13 Fold the short ties in half to form loops, then insert a loop upside down into each corner of the top seam. Pin in place, then stitch the top seam as before, sewing in the loops as you go. Turn the hat right side out so that the loops pop up out of each top corner.

14 Join the center back seam of the cuff as before. Fold the cuff in half lengthwise, wrong sides together, and pin both edges of the cuff onto the bottom right side edge of the crown so that all three edges are aligned. Stitch as before, then turn down the cuff.

15 Trim any loose ends of thread, then press the hat so that all the seams are flat, gently reshaping it if necessary. Thread the long tie through the loops and knot each end. Form the tie into a bow, pulling in the sides of the hat.

15

russian hat

THIS HAT IS FLATTERING TO MOST FACE SHAPES AND HAIRSTYLES. THE HAND-EMBROIDERED CORSAGE IS DETACHABLE AND CAN BE PINNED ONTO A FAVORITE CARDIGAN OR JACKET. IF YOU PREFER, YOU COULD OMIT THE CORSAGE ALTOGETHER AND DECORATE THE HAT WITH APPLIQUÉ AND EMBROIDERY; LOOK AT OTHER PROJECTS IN THIS BOOK FOR INSPIRATION.

MATERIALS

- ♥ 28 x 22 in. (70 x 55 cm) piece of black felted knitting
- ♥ small pieces of felted knitting or felt in three shades of red and pink
- ♥ small pieces of green felted knitting or felt
- ♥ polyester sewing threads in matching colors
- ♥ tapestry yarn in toning shades of red, pink, and green
- ♥ 1¹/₄ in. (3 cm) diameter red button
- ♥ 1¹/₄ in. (3 cm) long pin back

EQUIPMENT

- ♥ tape measure
- ♥ cardstock, pencil, ruler, and compass to make patterns and templates
- ♥ scissors—paper, fabric, and embroidery
- ♥ flat flower or glass-headed pins
- ♥ tapestry needle
- ♥ sewing needle
- ♥ thimble
- ♥ sewing machine or serger
- ♥ steam iron and pressing cloth

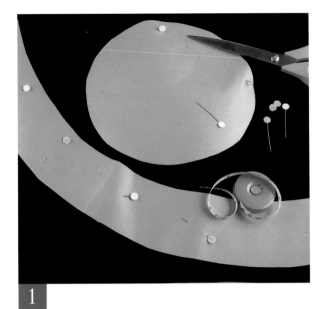

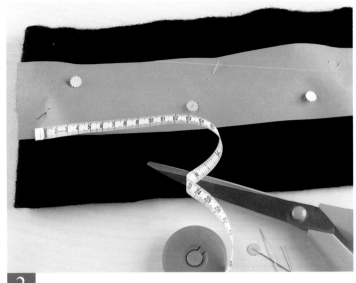

1 Enlarge the patterns on page 116 for the crown, side, and cuff of the hat. Measure the circumference of the head and adjust the length of the cuff (which is half the circumference of the head) and the short curved edge of the side section if necessary, remembering to allow ¹/₄ in. (5 mm) for seam allowances. Pin the crown and side patterns onto the black felt, making best use of the fabric available, and cut out.

2 Fold the remaining black felt in half widthwise. Pin the cuff onto the felt so that a shorter edge aligns with the fold and cut out.

Use felted knitting only for the hat—it is more flexible and giving than store-bought felt

MAKING UP

3 Select a stretch stitch such as double overlock or zigzag, or use a serger, to sew the hat pieces together. Pin the short ends of the side section right sides together and stitch using a ¹/₈ in. (3 mm) seam allowance and matching sewing thread. Pin the crown of the hat to the top edge of the side section (long curved edge), right sides together. Stitch, then turn right side out.

4

5

6

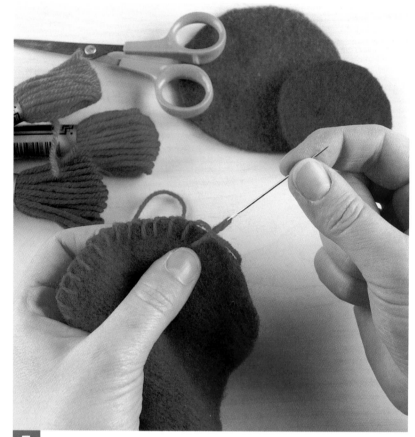

7

4 Pin the short ends of the cuff right sides together and stitch. Fold the cuff in half lengthwise, wrong sides together, and pin both edges of the cuff onto the bottom right side edge of the crown (short curved edge), so that all three edges and the seams are aligned. Stitch as before, then turn down the cuff.

5 Trim any loose ends of thread, then press the hat, taking care to roll out the seam around the crown with your fingers. Gently pull the hat into shape if necessary.

CORSAGE

6 Make templates for the corsage. Use a compass to draw $4^1/_2$, $3^1/_2$, and $2^1/_2$ in. (12, 9, and 6 cm) diameter circles. Also draw a $4^1/_2$ in. (12 cm) long leaf shape. Pin the circular templates onto the red and pink felt and cut out. Cut out two leaves from green felt.

7 Hand embroider around each circle using buttonhole stitch and tapestry yarn in toning shades.

8

9

10

8 Sew veins onto the leaf using stab stitch and a contrasting shade of tapestry yarn. Pin and sew the two leaves together using buttonhole stitch and toning tapestry yarn.

9 Layer the three circles together and stitch together through the center using matching sewing thread. Manipulate the circles to form a flower by stitching tucks on the reverse sides of each circle. Stitch a button to the center of the flower.

10 Using matching sewing thread, stitch one end of the leaf to the center back of the flower. Sew a pin back to the reverse of the leaf. Trim any loose ends of thread, then pin the corsage onto the hat.

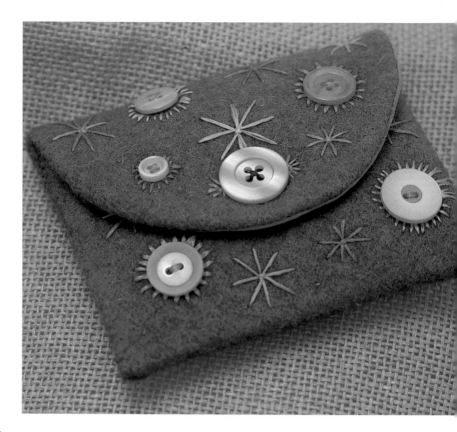

THIS SIMPLE PURSE WITH A FLAP AND BUTTON FASTENING IS VERY EASY TO MAKE. RAID YOUR BUTTON BOX, CHOOSING YOUR FAVORITES IN A VARIETY OF SIZES TO HIGHLIGHT AND EMBELLISH WITH HAND EMBROIDERY. THE LUSTROUS RAYON THREAD AND SILK LINING CONTRAST BEAUTIFULLY WITH THE MATTE FELT.

star and button purse

HOW LONG?
embroidery: **2 evenings**
construction: **2 hours**

MATERIALS
- ♥ $6^1/2$ x 13 in. (16.5 x 33 cm) piece of blue felted knitting or felt
- ♥ $6^1/2$ x 13 in. (16.5 x 33 cm) piece of orange silk for lining
- ♥ 12 orange buttons in different sizes, plus one for the fastening
- ♥ basting thread in a contrasting color
- ♥ blue polyester sewing thread
- ♥ rayon embroidery threads in shades of orange (three different brands are used here to increase textural contrast)
- ♥ 2 x 1 in. (5 x 2.5 cm) piece of iron-on interfacing

EQUIPMENT
- ♥ cardstock, pencil, ruler, and compass to make pattern
- ♥ scissors—paper, fabric, and embroidery
- ♥ flat flower or glass-headed pins
- ♥ embroidery needle
- ♥ sewing needle
- ♥ thimble
- ♥ sewing machine
- ♥ steam iron and pressing cloth

This fun purse uses buttons for decoration as well as for a simple fastening

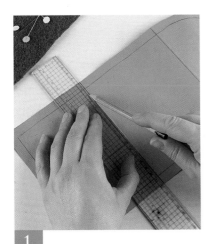

1

2

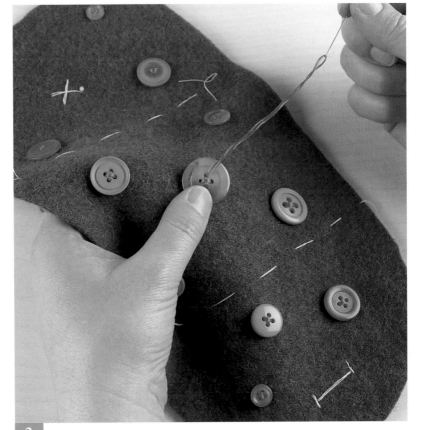

3

1 Draw a 6¹/₂ x 13 in. (16.5 x 33 cm) rectangle onto cardstock. Draw a curve inside one end of the rectangle to form the flap of the purse. Cut out the pattern and fold to determine where the folds in the purse will be. Mark the folds, seam allowance, button, and buttonhole position onto the pattern. Pin the pattern onto the felt and cut out.

2 Baste a row of stitches along each fold line on the felt, then use basting stitches to indicate the positions of the button and buttonhole.

3 Using a doubled strand of rayon embroidery thread, sew buttons all over the felt, avoiding the basting stitches and seam allowance.

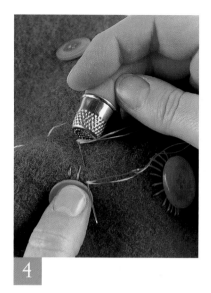

4

5

4 Using doubled strands of embroidery thread in different shades, decorate around each button using stab stitch. Use each shade evenly across the purse.

5 Hand embroider between the buttons using star stitch. Again, use each shade evenly across the purse and avoid the basting stitches.

6 Attach a small piece of iron-on interfacing to the reverse side of the felt where the buttonhole will be situated to ensure you have a firm area on which to stitch later.

7 Using the embroidered felt as a template, cut out a piece of lining fabric to match (the embroidery may have distorted the shape of the felt slightly, so do not use the original pattern as a template). Pin the lining to the felt, wrong sides together.

6

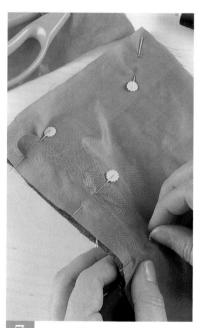

7

8

MAKING UP

8 Machine sew around the edge using a ¹/₂ in. (1 cm) seam allowance and sewing thread. Leave a 4 in. (10 cm) opening at the straight end. Trim the seam allowance to ¹/₄ in. (5 mm). Turn right side out and close the opening using slip stitch. Press well, rolling out the edges with your fingers.

9 Machine stitch the buttonhole through the felt and lining, making sure that the hole is slightly larger than the fastening button. Slit through the hole with embroidery scissors, then decorate with buttonhole stitch using a doubled strand of embroidery thread.

9

10

10 Fold the purse along the basting stitches and pin in place. Using sewing thread, overcast the side edges of the purse together. At the top of the seams, make several very firm stitches. Remove the basting stitches, then press the purse along the folds.

11 Check the position of the fastening button and sew in place using sewing thread.

11

35

Felted knitting provides ideal cushioning for delicate items, such as reading glasses

MATERIALS

♥ *9 x 7 in. (23 x 18 cm) pieces of red and white felted knitting or felt*

♥ *7 x 7 in. (18 x 18 cm) piece of white felted knitting or felt*

♥ *fine woolen embroidery threads in red and white*

♥ *basting thread in a contrasting color*

EQUIPMENT

♥ *cardstock, pencil, ruler, and compass to make patterns and templates*

♥ *scissors—paper, fabric, and embroidery*

♥ *flat flower or glass-headed pins*

♥ *embroidery needle*

♥ *thimble*

♥ *steam iron and pressing cloth*

glasses case

THIS HAND-STITCHED GLASSES CASE IS BASED ON A TRADITIONAL SWEDISH DESIGN AND COMBINES THE PERENNIALLY FAVORITE MOTIFS OF HEARTS AND FLOWERS.

 MAKING UP IS VERY EASY—THE CASE IS SIMPLY A SQUARE OF FABRIC THAT IS EMBROIDERED AND THEN FOLDED AND STITCHED INTO A POUCH SHAPE.

HOW LONG?
embroidery: **2 evenings**
construction: $^1/_2$ **hour**

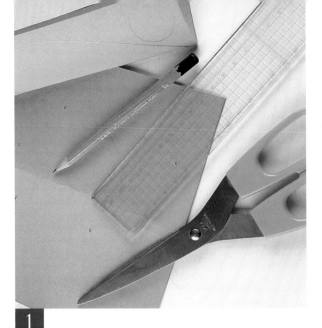

1 Draw a 7 in. (18 cm) square onto cardstock, adding a small curve in the top two corners, to form the case pattern. Fold a $3^1/2$ x $6^1/2$ in. (9 x 17 cm) piece of cardstock in half lengthwise and draw long half heart shape. Draw a 1 in. (2.5 cm) diameter circle in the bottom corner using a compass. Cut out all the pieces.

2 Pin the case pattern onto the white felt and cut out. Pinning the templates onto the felt, cut out two red hearts, six red circles, and six white circles.

3 Fold the white felt in half so that the curved and right-angled corners align and mark the center fold using basting stitches. Pin a heart onto each half of the case with the curved edges at the top. Pin a red circle above the center of each heart and on either side of the bottom of each heart. Trim the circles to fit if necessary, but try to keep the design symmetrical.

4 Hand sew the hearts and circles in place using buttonhole stitch and two strands of white embroidery thread.

5 Pin the white circles onto the top curves and center of the hearts, trimming them symmetrically to fit if necessary. Hand sew in place using buttonhole stitch and two strands of red embroidery thread.

6 Using two strands of thread for all the embellishment, embroider inside the white circles using star stitch and red thread, then add stab stitches in the center to complete the flower heads. Use white thread and back stitch to form flower stems and lazy daisy stitch to indicate leaves. Embroider the red circles using star stitch and white thread. Fill in other areas with cross stitch and star stitch using contrasting colored thread.

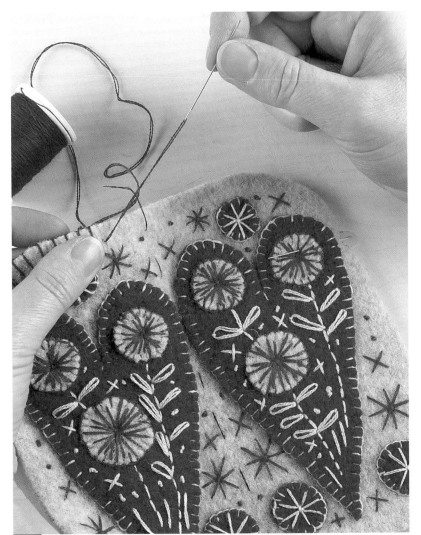

MAKING UP

7 Mark with pins where the opening will be, extending about 2 in. (5 cm) below the top curved edges. Hand embroider around the opening edge with buttonhole stitch using two strands of red embroidery thread.

8 Fold the case along the basting stitches, wrong sides together, and pin in place. Using two strands of red embroidery thread, sew the bottom and side edges using buttonhole stitch. Remove the basting stitches, trim any loose ends of thread, and press.

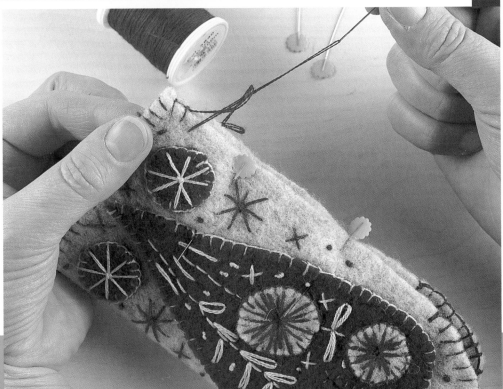

39

lavender needle case

HOW LONG?

embroidery: **1 evening**

construction: **2 hours**

GARDENS WERE THE INSPIRATION FOR THIS NEEDLE CASE, AS WAS A FAVORITE CHILDHOOD SONG, "LAVENDERS BLUE." THE CASE IS MADE IN THE FORM OF A BOOK, WITH A COVER DECORATED IN SOFT BLUES, PURPLES, AND GREENS, AND SEVERAL FELT PAGES INSIDE FOR PINNING NEEDLES. THE MOTIFS ARE MACHINE EMBROIDERED AND THE CASE IS FINISHED BY HAND USING BUTTONHOLE STITCH AROUND THE EDGES.

MATERIALS

♥ *12 x 5 in. (30 x 12.5 cm) piece of dark blue felted knitting or felt*

♥ *small pieces of felted knitting or felt in shades of blue, purple, and green for the pages and motifs*

♥ *polyester sewing threads in matching colors*

♥ *rayon hand and machine embroidery threads in toning colors*

♥ *20 in. (50 cm) length of blue rayon cord*

♥ *basting thread in a contrasting color*

EQUIPMENT

♥ *cardstock, pencil, and ruler to make templates*

♥ *scissors—paper, fabric, and embroidery*

♥ *flat flower or glass-headed pins*

♥ *medium and large tapestry needles*

♥ *thimble*

♥ *sewing machine*

♥ *steam iron and pressing cloth*

1

2

3

4

in the same way. Cut two lavender flowers in different shades of blue and one light purple heart.

3 Fold the dark blue cover in half widthwise and mark the fold using basting stitches. Pin the heart in the center of the left-hand section, leaving a little more space near the spine of the book. Pin the lavender flowers and stems onto the right-hand section so that the stems cross each other. Machine sew in place using zigzag stitch and matching sewing thread.

4 Cut a small sliver of light and dark purple felt and pin them to the center of the lavender flowers. Cut down the heart template to about half size, then cut out a small heart from dark purple felt. Pin and stitch it to the center of the large purple heart.

1 Draw a 5 x 4 in. (12.5 x 10 cm) rectangle onto cardstock and cut out. Pinning the template onto the felt, cut out three pieces in different colors for the pages. Make a 12 x 5 in. (30 x 12.5 cm) template for the needle case cover (if your dark blue felt is larger than this) and cut out one piece.

2 Cut two $3^{1}/_2$ x $^{1}/_4$ in. (9 cm x 5 mm) strips of felt in different shades of green to form stems. Fold a piece of cardstock in half and draw a $3^{1}/_2$ in. (9 cm) long half heart shape onto it and cut out. Make a $2^{3}/_4$ in. (7 cm) long lavender flower template

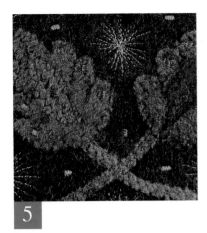

5

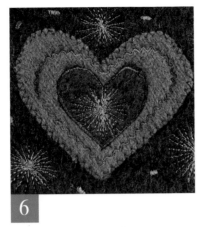

6

7

5 Machine embroider small dots of satin stitch around the edges of the flowers in a toning color of rayon embroidery thread. Choose a decorative stitch on your machine to embroider the center of each flower using a different color thread.

6 Use a narrow satin stitch to outline the smaller heart, then stitch around the larger heart using a decorative machine embroidery stitch. Stitch a star in the center. Decorate the background of the needle case using machine-stitched stars and satin stitch dots.

7 Using buttonhole stitch, hand embroider around the edges of the cover and pages with rayon embroidery thread in toning colors. Trim any loose ends of thread and press all the pieces.

MAKING UP

8 Stack the pages one on top of the other and place inside the folded case. Pin in place. Using a large needle and rayon cord, make a large stitch through all the layers from the front to the back and then up again to the front. If you have a problem pulling the needle through, use a hole punch or an awl to prepare holes in the correct places. Remove the needle and tie a bow in the cord.

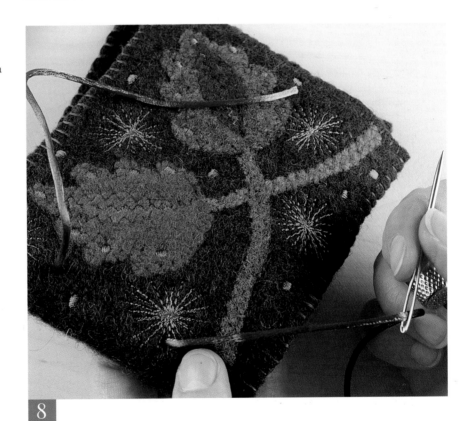

8

starburst handbag

HOW LONG?

embroidery: **3-4 evenings**

construction: **2 hours**

THIS SMALL HANDBAG IS APPLIQUED WITH CIRCLES AND DECORATED WITH A VARIETY OF HAND EMBROIDERY STITCHES IN SHINY RAYON THREADS AND RETRO BUTTONS GLEANED FROM THRIFT SHOPS. THE BAG HAS BOX CORNERS AND IS CLOSED WITH A MAGNETIC CLASP. THE SHAPE IS KEPT SIMPLE TO SHOW OFF THE DECORATION. IT IS AN IDEAL PROJECT FOR THOSE WHO HAVE MASTERED SOME SIMPLE HAND EMBROIDERY STITCHES AND FEEL READY TO HAVE FUN MAKING A LARGER PROJECT.

MATERIALS

♥ *32 x 14 in. (80 x 40 cm) piece of dark pink felted knitting or felt*

♥ *small pieces of felted knitting or felt in shades of red, pink, and green*

♥ *polyester sewing threads in matching colors*

♥ *rayon hand embroidery threads in matching colors*

♥ *selection of small buttons in red, pink, and green*

♥ *magnetic clasp*

EQUIPMENT

♥ *cardstock, pencil, ruler, and compass to make templates*

♥ *scissors—fabric, embroidery, and paper*

♥ *flat flower or glass-headed pins*

♥ *large-eyed mbroidery needles*

♥ *sewing machine*

♥ *serger(optional)*

hand embroidery stitches can be
effective worked in an array of
rayon threads

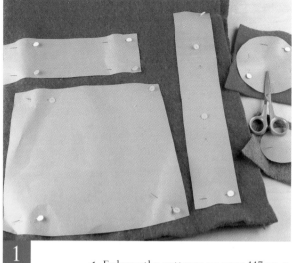

1

3

1 Enlarge the patterns on page 117 on a photocopier. Fold the dark pink felt in half widthwise and pin the pieces on it. Cut out, making sure the top band is placed on the fold. Use a compass to draw 5, 2$\frac{1}{2}$, 2$\frac{1}{4}$, and 1$\frac{1}{2}$ in. (13, 6.5, 6, and 3.5 cm) diameter circles onto cardstock. Cut out two large, five each of the two medium circles, and four small circles in shades of red, pink, and green.

2 Mark the fold at the bottom of the bag by making a line of pins 1 in. (2.5 cm) up from the bottom of the main piece, front and back. Pin the two large circles to the front and back of the bag. Pin smaller circles into the central circles and in the center of two of the smaller circles on each side.

3 Using short lengths of hand embroidery thread, appliqué the large circle onto the background using buttonhole stitch.

4 Appliqué a smaller circle into the centre of the larger circle, then sew a button into the center.

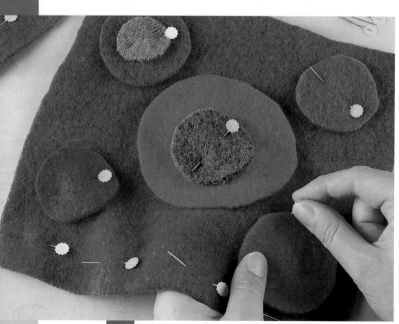

2

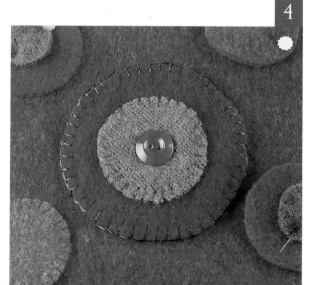

4

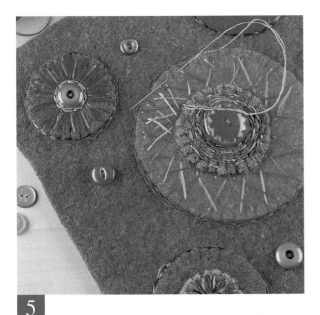

5

6

MAKING UP

7 Press the bag panels and pin right sides together. Select a stretch stitch, such as an overlock or zigzag stitch on your sewing machine, or use a serger to stitch around the bottom three edges. Stitch right on the edge of the fabric as the seam allowance is only $^1/_4$ in (5 mm).

8 To make a flat bottom, fold and pin the side seam to the bottom seam at each corner $1^1/_2$ in. (4 cm) in from the edge. Stitch across the corner at an angle of 45 degrees using an overlock or stretch stitch and trim close to the stitching. Turn the bag the right way out.

7

5 Using hand embroidery thread in a range of colors, decorate each circle using running stitch, stab stitch, lazy daisy stitch, herringbone stitch and cross stitch. Outline some of the buttons and circles with chain stitch.

6 Stitch random buttons between the circles and sew around these with stab stitch. Fill in the remaining areas with more decorative stitches, such as star stitch and cross stitch.

8

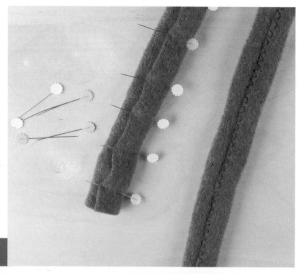

9

11 Take the top band and join it into a circle by stitching the two ends together using the serger or a stretch stitch.

12 Fit the magnetic clasp in place following the manufacturer's instructions. Fit one half over the back seam $1/2$ in. (1 cm) in from the edge and the other half exactly opposite at the center of the band.

11

12

10

9 Fold the handles lengthwise so that the edges meet in the center. Pin and stitch down the middle using a stretch stitch on the sewing machine.

10 Position the handles upside down on the right side of the bag, with the ends of each handle at the top of the bag. Make sure the handles are evenly placed on both sides of the bag. The ends should protrude slightly from the top. Pin them in place.

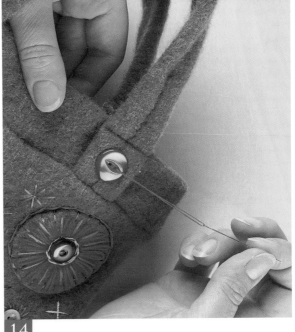

13 Fold the top band in half lengthwise, wrong sides together and right sides out. Pin the two edges of the band to the right side top edge of the bag, making sure the edges are aligned and that the magnetic clasp is correctly positioned. As there are now five layers of felt to stitch through, test your machine first to make sure it can cope. If it can, stitch around the top edge using an overlock or stretch stitch. If your machine will not stitch this many layers, hand stitch the layers together using buttonhole stitch.

14 Trim the ends of the handles so they are flush. Turn the band up so that the sides of the magnetic clasp meet and flip up the handles. Fix the base of each handle to the bag with a few stitches by hand or machine and sew a button there.

15 Roll the seams out with your fingers, then press carefully with a steam iron and a cloth .

tote bag

HOW LONG?
embroidery: **2 evenings**
construction: **3 hours**

THIS BAG IS AN IDEAL PROJECT FOR RECYCLING AN OLD SWEATER OR OTHER SUITABLY SIZED GARMENT. THE BAG SHAPE WAS INSPIRED BY THE DESIGNS OF THE 1950S, AND HAS BEEN EMBELLISHED WITH MACHINE APPLIQUÉ AND EMBROIDERY. YOU COULD TAKE THE RETRO FEEL A STAGE FURTHER BY DECORATING THE BAG WITH HAND EMBROIDERY STITCHES AND VINTAGE BUTTONS. THE HANDLE IS CUT AS PART OF THE MAIN PANEL TO PRODUCE A PLEASING SHAPE.

MATERIALS

- ♥ *28 x 18 in. (70 x 45 cm) piece of dark green felted knitting or felt*
- ♥ *small pieces of felted knitting or felt in shades of purple, pink, red, and aqua*
- ♥ *28 x 18 in. (70 x 45 cm) piece of pink silk for lining*
- ♥ *polyester sewing threads in matching colors*
- ♥ *rayon machine embroidery threads in toning colors*
- ♥ *basting thread in a contrasting color*

EQUIPMENT

- ♥ *cardstock, pencil, ruler, and compass to make templates*
- ♥ *scissors—fabric, embroidery, and paper*
- ♥ *flat flower or glass-headed pins*
- ♥ *sewing needle*
- ♥ *sewing machine with free-motion embroidery function*
- ♥ *steam iron and pressing cloth*

Use the bag as a handbag or a tote in which to store your knitting

1 Enlarge the pattern on page 118 on a photocopier so that it measures 13 x 17 in. (33 x 43 cm) at the widest and longest points. Fold the dark green felt in half widthwise. Pin the pattern onto the felt and cut out to make two identical pieces.

2 Use a compass to draw 3¹/₂, 3, and 2 in. (9, 7.5, and 5 cm) diameter circles and a small semicircular petal shape onto cardstock and cut out. Pinning the templates onto the felt, cut out two circles of each size in shades of red and pink. Cut out 22 petals in shades of red and pink (enough to fit around both the largest circles). Make leaf shape templates in various sizes and cut out eight leaves in shades of aqua and green.

3 Pin the largest circle in the center of one bag panel just below the handle. Arrange the petals around it. Cut a thin strip of green or aqua felt and pin it in place to form a stem. Pin a pair of leaves at the base of the stem. Pin the remaining circles on either side with stems and a single leaf to form a pleasing design. Repeat a similar composition with the remaining pieces on the back panel. Machine sew the pieces in place using zigzag stitch and matching sewing thread.

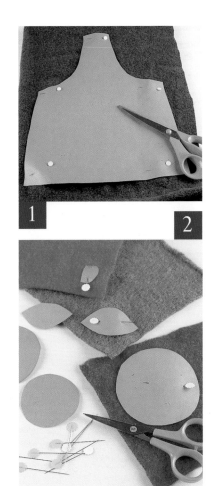

4 Cut down the circle templates by 2 in. (5 cm) in diameter and cut out small circles of red and pink to form the centers of the flowers. Sew in place as before.

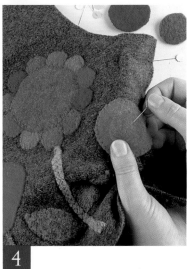

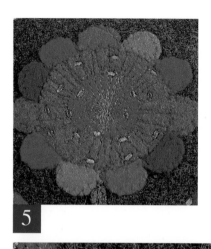

5

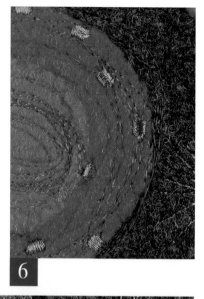

6

7

5 Using rayon embroidery thread, machine embroider a star into the center flower and embellish with satin stitch dots in different colors.

6 Using free-motion embroidery, stitch circles in different colors in the inner and outer sections of the left-hand flower. Decorate the outer section with satin stitch dots. Decorate the outer section of the right-hand flower in the same way, but decorate the inner section of the flower with a star.

7 Embroider veins onto the leaves using straight stitch. Decorate the spaces around the flowers using star stitch. Repeat the embroidery embellishment on the back panel of the tote bag, varying the details as you wish.

MAKING UP

8 Press the bag panels and pin right sides together. Using straight stitch and matching sewing thread, machine sew around the sides and base of the bag and the top of the handle with a $^{1}/_{2}$ in. (1 cm) seam allowance.

8

9

9 Fold the lining fabric in half widthwise and pin the bag onto it. Using the bag as a template, cut out two pieces of lining. (The embroidery may have distorted the shape of the felt slightly, so do not use the original pattern as a template.) Place the lining pieces right sides together and machine sew the sides, base, and top of the handle using straight stitch and matching sewing thread. Trim the seam allowance on the bag and lining to ¼ in. (5 mm).

10 Turn the felt bag right side out and press carefully, rolling out the seams with your fingers and gently pulling it into shape. Carefully fold in and press ½ in. (1 cm) along the top opening edges of the felt and lining. Place the lining inside the felt bag, wrong sides together. Pin and baste the top edges together so that felt is slightly raised above the lining.

10

11 Machine sew in place using straight stitch. Make sure the threads match the lining and felt, using a different color for the top thread and bobbin. Remove the basting stitches, trim any loose ends of thread, and press.

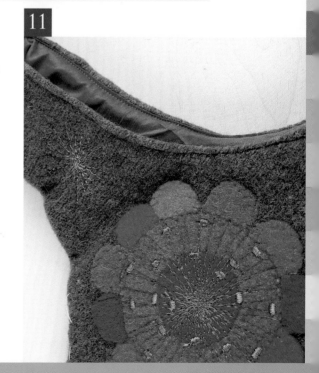

11

flower mittens

HOW LONG?
embroidery: **2–3 evenings**
construction: **1 hour**

THESE CUTE MITTENS FEATURE FLORAL HAND EMBROIDERY, WITH BUTTONS FORMING THE CENTER OF THE FLOWERS. THIS PROJECT IS AN EXCELLENT OPPORTUNITY TO REUSE AN OLD FAVORITE SWEATER, BY CUTTING OUT THE MITTENS FROM THE SLEEVES OF THE FELTED MATERIAL, ALTHOUGH YOU CAN OF COURSE USE ANY PIECE OF FELTED KNITTING.

Assorted buttons form the basis for simple flower motifs on these fun mittens

MATERIALS

- ♥ *12 x 29 in. (30 x 74 cm) piece of blue felted knitting*
- ♥ *small pieces of felted knitting in reds, pinks, and oranges*
- ♥ *selection of small buttons in toning colors of red, pink, and orange*
- ♥ *blue polyester sewing thread*
- ♥ *fine embroidery thread in toning colors including yellow and green*

EQUIPMENT

- ♥ *cardstock, pencil, and compass to make patterns and templates*
- ♥ *scissors—paper, fabric, and embroidery*
- ♥ *flat flower or glass-headed pins*
- ♥ *embroidery needle*
- ♥ *thimble*
- ♥ *sewing machine*
- ♥ *steam iron and pressing cloth*

1

1 Place your hand onto a piece of cardstock with fingers together and thumb slightly apart. Draw around your hand and 2 in. (5 cm) down below your wrist. Round off the top of the finger and thumb sections to get a good basic mitten

shape. Make sure the opening at the wrist is $^1/_2$-1 in. (1-2.5 cm) wider than the wrist to allow the hand to get through. Add a $^1/_2$ in. (1 cm) seam allowance all around, then cut out the pattern.

2 Fold the blue felt in half widthwise. Pin the pattern onto the fabric and cut out. Repeat for the second mitten. If you want to recycle a sweater, position the pattern at the end of each sleeve so that the cuff of the sleeve will form the wristband of the mitten and cut out; the side seams of the mittens will already be joined (see the green example in the photograph).

2

3

4

5

6

3 Make sure you have a top and an underside for each hand, with the right side of the fabric outermost, if discernible. Make a 1¹/₄ in. (3 cm) diameter circle template and cut out 10 small circles in shades of red, pink, and orange felt. Pin five circles onto the top section of each mitten in an asymmetrical design.

4 Using doubled strands of embroidery thread in toning colors, appliqué each circle in place with buttonhole stitch.

5 Sew a small button onto the center of each circle using a doubled strand of embroidery thread in a contrasting color.

6 Sew stems from the buttons down toward the wrist using back stitch. Form leaves using stab stitch and lazy daisy stitch. Combine

yellow stems with green leaves, and vice versa. Fill in the remaining spaces with star, cross, and French knot stitches in a variety of colors.

MAKING UP

7 Place the top and underside pieces of each mitten right sides together and pin around the edge, leaving the wrist open. Using straight stitch and polyester sewing thread, machine sew around the edges using a ¹/₂ in. (1 cm) seam allowance. Trim the seam to ¹/₄ in. (5 mm). Turn the gloves right side out, using a knitting needle or pencil to help turn out the thumb.

8 Turn the cuff hem to the inside by ¹/₂ in. (1 cm). Select a stretch stitch, such as double overlock or zigzag, then machine sew the hem in place. Decorate the wrist opening using a doubled strand of embroidery thread in a contrasting color and buttonhole stitch. Trim any loose ends of thread, then carefully press the mittens, rolling out the seams with your fingers and easing them into shape.

HOW LONG?

embroidery: **2 evenings**

construction: **4 hours**

MATERIALS

- ♥ *24 x 24 in. (60 x 60 cm) piece of charcoal gray extra-thick felted knitting; adjust quantity for your foot size if necessary*
- ♥ *black extra-strong polyester sewing thread*
- ♥ *red rayon embroidery thread*
- ♥ *two small red buttons*
- ♥ *small amount of polyester batting*
- ♥ *basting thread in a contrasting color*
- ♥ *latex glue (optional)*

EQUIPMENT

- ♥ *tape measure*
- ♥ *cardstock, pencil, ruler, and compass to make patterns and templates*
- ♥ *scissors——paper, fabric, and embroidery*
- ♥ *masking tape (if you need to adjust size of pattern)*
- ♥ *flat flower or glass-headed pins*
- ♥ *embroidery needle*
- ♥ *thimble*
- ♥ *sewing machine*
- ♥ *steam iron and pressing cloth*
- ♥ *tissue paper and paintbrush (optional)*

oriental slippers

THESE SLIPPERS ARE MADE FROM LAMBSWOOL FELTED KNITTING THAT HAS BEEN WASHED AT 140° F (60°C) INSTEAD OF THE USUAL 90°F (30°C) THAT IS SUITABLE FOR MOST PROJECTS. THIS PRODUCES AN EXTRA-THICK FELT THAT IS VERY DURABLE. DEPENDING ON THE TYPE OF YARN YOU USE, YOU MAY NEED TO WASH IT ONCE OR TWICE TO GET THE THICKNESS REQUIRED. IF YOU HAVE A PIECE OF VERY THICK FELT OR A SWEATER THAT HAS OVERSHRUNK AND IS TOO THICK FOR ANOTHER PROJECT, THEY MAY BE IDEAL FOR THIS. BEFORE YOU START, CHECK THAT YOUR SEWING MACHINE CAN COPE WITH TWO LAYERS OF VERY THICK FABRIC AND USE A DENIM OR STRONG NEEDLE. THE SLIPPERS ARE SIMPLY DECORATED WITH HAND EMBROIDERED STARS, POM-POMS, AND BUTTONS.

Boldly colored hand embroidered stars and chunky pom-poms lend these slippers an eastern feel

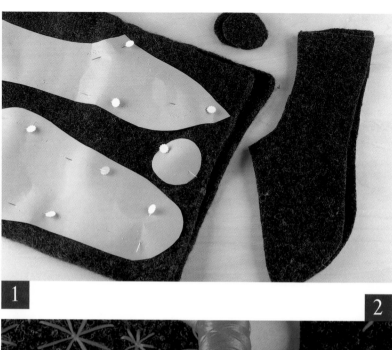

1 Enlarge the side and sole patterns on page 119 on a photocopier. Draw a 2 in. (5 cm) diameter circle for the pom-pom. Cut out all the pieces. Measure the length of your foot and adjust the side and sole pieces if necessary by shortening or lengthening them at the lines indicated. Also measure the width of your foot and adjust as necessary. Fix alterations in place with masking tape. Also measure the width of your sole and adjust as necessary. Measure the width of your foot across the widest part, not including the sole. Divide this figure in two and adjust the side piece at the point indicated if necessary. Add a $^1/_2$ in. (1 cm) seam allowance around all the pattern pieces except the circles for the pom-poms. Fold the felt in half and pin the pattern pieces onto it. Cut out the pieces so that you have a left and right sole and four side pieces, plus four circles for the pom-poms.

2 Make sure you have the correct pieces for each foot, then mark each piece with basting thread so that you know which is the outermost side. Hand embroider each piece using star stitch in different sizes and a doubled strand of rayon thread. Space the stars evenly across the felt but avoid the seam allowances. Make two pom-poms following the instructions on page 77. Decorate them with red buttons, cross stitches, and buttonhole stitch.

3

MAKING UP

3 Press all the pieces. Place pairs of side pieces wrong sides together and pin the upper and back seams. Machine sew using straight stitch and sewing thread. Trim the seams to ¹/₄ in. (5 mm).

4 With wrong sides together, pin the soles to the completed upper sections. Sew the seams and trim as before.

5 Decorate around all the seams and the opening edges using buttonhole stitch and a doubled strand of rayon embroidery thread.

6 Sew a pom-pom to each slipper at the top of the center seam using sewing thread. Trim any loose ends of thread. If you want to give the slippers a nonslip sole, fill them with rolled tissue paper to hold their shape, then turn them over and paint the soles with latex glue. Allow to dry, then repeat this process two more times.

4

5

6

To make a recycled version of this case, use the end of a sweater sleeve, using the cuff as the opening

MATERIALS
- ♥ 8 x 8 in. (20 x 20 cm) piece of dark blue felted knitting or felt
- ♥ small pieces of felted knitting or felt in two shades of red
- ♥ red and blue polyester sewing thread
- ♥ rayon embroidery thread in two matching shades of red
- ♥ ³/₄ in. (2 cm) square of hook-and-loop fastening tape (such as Velcro)
- ♥ 35 in. (90 cm) length of red rayon cord

EQUIPMENT
- ♥ cardstock, pencil, and ruler to make templates
- ♥ scissors—paper, fabric, and embroidery
- ♥ flat flower or glass-headed pins
- ♥ sewing needle
- ♥ thimble
- ♥ sewing machine with free-motion embroidery function
- ♥ steam iron and pressing cloth

ipod case

MAKE THIS SMALL PROTECTIVE CASE TO CARRY YOUR iPOD SAFELY AROUND YOUR NECK. IT HAS A HOOK-AND-LOOP FASTENING FOR ADDED SAFETY, AND IS DECORATED WITH AN APPLIQUÉD HEART AND MACHINE EMBROIDERY STITCHES. IF YOUR SEWING MACHINE DOES NOT HAVE A FREE-MOTION EMBROIDERY FUNCTION, EMBROIDER THE CASE WITH DIFFERENT STITCH DESIGNS.

HOW LONG?
embroidery: **1-2 hours**
construction: **¹/₂ hours**

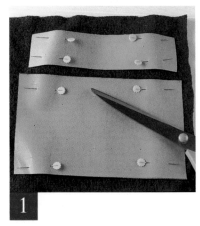

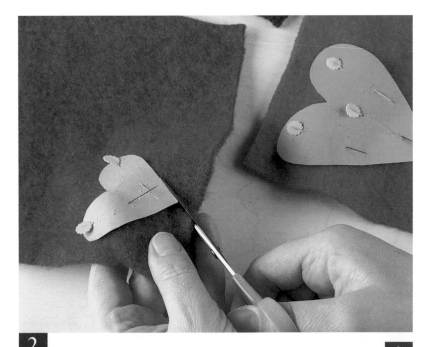

2

3

1 Draw 8 x 5 in. (20 x 12.5 cm) and 7½ x 2 in. (19 x 5 cm) rectangles onto cardstock. Cut out the templates, pin them onto the dark blue felt, and cut out.

2 Fold a 4 in. (10 cm) square of cardstock in half and draw a half heart shape. Repeat using a 2 in. (5 cm) square of cardstock. Cut out the templates, pin one to each shade of red felt, and cut out.

3 Pin the large heart in the center of the largest blue piece, leaving slightly more space above the heart than below it. Stitch around the edges of the heart using zigzag stitch and matching sewing thread. Place the second heart inside the first. Pin and stitch in place as before.

4

5

6

4 Using free-motion machine embroidery, stitch freely over the heart shapes using toning colors of rayon embroidery threads.

5 Continue using free-motion embroidery in small circular movements to form dots over the background with rayon embroidery thread.

MAKING UP

6 Fold the decorated section in half widthwise, right sides together, and pin the seam. Select a stretch stitch such as double overlock or zigzag, and machine sew the seam with blue sewing thread. Stitch right on the edge of the fabric as the seam allowance is $^1/_4$ in. (5 mm). Refold so that the seam is at center back and pin the bottom seam together. Stitch as before. Fold the top band piece in half widthwise, right sides together, and sew the seam as for the main panel.

7

7 Hand stitch one section of the hook-and-loop fastening onto the right side of the top band, about ¹/₄ in. (5 mm) from the top edge and covering the center back seam. Stitch the other section onto the center front of the band. Fold the band in half and check that the two pieces align; adjust if necessary.

8 Turn the main piece right side out. Fold the top band in half lengthwise, wrong sides together, and pin both edges of the top band onto the top right side edge of the main piece so that all three edges are aligned. Make sure that both sections of the hook-and-loop fastening are facing outward. Stitch as before and trim any loose ends of thread.

9 Press carefully, rolling out the seams using your fingers. Tie a knot at each end of the rayon cord and stitch it to the inside seam of the top band using matching sewing thread. Fold the top band up so the hook-and-loop fastening aligns.

8

9

sapphire scarf

HOW LONG?

to machine knit the scarf: **1–2 hours**

embroidery: **1–2 evenings**

THIS SCARF SHOWS JUST HOW EFFECTIVE SIMPLE MOTIFS SUCH AS SQUARES CAN BE. THEY ARE LAYERED IN JEWEL COLORS AND THEN DECORATED WITH SHINY RAYON EMBROIDERY THREADS TO CREATE A RICHLY COLORED WINTER ACCESSORY. YOU CAN KNIT YOUR OWN LENGTH OF SCARF (SEE PAGE 12) OR RECYCLE A SCARF THAT IS SUITABLE FOR FELTING. ALTERNATELY, PATCH TOGETHER PIECES FROM RECYCLED GARMENTS USING A SERGER OR STRETCH STITCH ON YOUR SEWING MACHINE.

MATERIALS

♥ *70 x 12 in. (175 x 30 cm) piece of dark blue felted knitting*

♥ *small pieces of felted knitting in shades of blue, purple, and turquoise; you need enough for eighteen 2^1/$_2$ in. (6 cm) squares and eighteen 1^1/$_2$ in. (3.5 cm) squares*

♥ *polyester sewing thread in matching colors*

♥ *rayon embroidery thread in toning colors*

EQUIPMENT

♥ *cardstock, pencil, ruler, and compass to make patterns and templates*

♥ *scissors—paper, fabric, and embroidery*

♥ *flat flower or glass-headed pins*

♥ *sewing machine with free-motion embroidery function*

♥ *steam iron and pressing cloth*

1

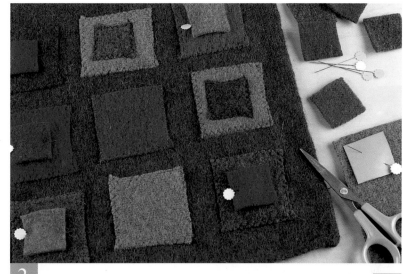

2

3

1 Draw a $2^{1}/_2$ in. (6 cm) and $1^{1}/_2$ in. (3.5 cm) square onto cardstock and cut out. Pin the templates onto the small pieces of blue, purple, and turquoise felt and cut out 18 of each size. Place nine large squares onto each end of the scarf in a grid formation, arranging the colors in a pleasing design. Pin in place and machine sew around the edges using matching sewing thread.

2 Pin and sew the smaller squares in the center of the larger ones, experimenting with the color placement first.

3 Using straight stitch and rayon embroidery thread, machine sew random lines of stitching up and down the sides of each large square. You will find this quicker if you use the reverse function on the machine. Inside alternate small squares, embroider a star using straight stitch. Using free-motion embroidery, add randomly sewn circles on the remaining small squares, using a different shade of embroidery thread. If your machine does not have a free-motion function, continue to embroider stars in different shades. Trim any loose ends of thread, then press the scarf.

Simple geometric shapes and a restricted palette produce striking results

free-form scarf

Scraps of felt sewn onto yarn make a fabulous raw material with which to knit a truly original scarf

HOW LONG?
making the yarn: **1–2 days**
knitting up: **1–2 days**

MATERIALS
♥ *small scraps of felted knitting or felt in various colors; you need enough to create about 750 strips*
♥ *148 yd. (150 m) 2-ply machine knitting yarn in 4 colors or 4-ply hand knitting yarn in two colors*
♥ *at least two 650 yd. (600 m) spools of rayon embroidery thread in two toning colors*

EQUIPMENT
♥ *embroidery or fabric scissors*
♥ *rotary cutter (optional)*
♥ *sewing machine*
♥ *pair of size 11 (7 mm) knitting needles*

IF YOU HAVE A SEWING MACHINE, YOU CAN DESIGN AND MAKE YOUR OWN ORIGINAL YARNS BY STITCHING SMALL STRIPS OF FELT ALONG ONE OR MORE LENGTHS OF ORDINARY KNITTING YARN. CHOOSE YOUR OWN COLOR COMBINATIONS TO CREATE YOUR OWN PIECE OF WEARABLE ART. THE "FELT YARN" IS KNITTED UP IN SPIDER STITCH TO PRODUCE A LOOPY FABRIC THAT DISPLAYS THE YARN TO ITS BEST ADVANTAGE. THE OTHER BENEFIT IS THAT YOUR SCARF WILL GROW IN LENGTH VERY QUICKLY. THIS IS ALSO A GREAT WAY OF USING UP SMALL SCRAPS OF FELT LEFT OVER FROM OTHER PROJECTS.

1

2

1 Cut strips of felt about 2^{1}/$_{2}$ in. (6 cm) long and ^{1}/$_{2}$ in. (1^{1}/$_{2}$ cm) wide. It is good to have a slight variation in the sizes. You will need about 750 strips. (Use a rotary cutter if you have one, to speed things up.)

2 Thread the sewing machine with one color of embroidery thread on the top and another in the bobbin. Set it to a wide zigzag stitch. Bring the yarns together under the foot of the machine. (Keep them in a box on the floor.) Stitch over the strands (two strands if using hand knitting yarn or four strands if using machine knitting yarn) to form a single yarn. Pull the yarn through from the back: the feed dog on the sewing machine will not be in contact to do this for you.

4 Using knitting needles and the felt yarn, cast on 20 stitches and work a row of plain knitting. On the second row, work a row of spider stitch by inserting the right-hand needle into the first stitch. Wind the yarn anti-clockwise around both needles, then around the right-hand needle only.

5 Pull the right-hand needle back and take the yarn through to create a new stitch, which will be much longer than the others. Slip the old stitch off the needle. Continue along the row. Work alternate rows of plain knitting and spider stitch until you have 1 yd. (1 m) of yarn left. Cast off with the remaining yarn.

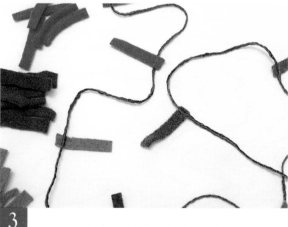

3 Attach felt strips in random colors at 8 in. (20 cm) intervals by lifting the foot and stitching over the felt and onto the yarn. Wind the yarn into balls and you will end up with about four 6 in. (15 cm) balls.

rose accessories

HOW LONG?
machine stitching: $^1/_2$ **hour**
hand stitching: 1 **hour**

THIS PROJECT CAN EASILY BE ADAPTED TO CREATE A NUMBER OF SMALL ACCESSORIES, SUCH AS A PIN, CHOKER, OR HAIR DECORATION, AND IS A GREAT WAY TO USE UP SMALL SCRAPS OF FELT. THE ROSE IS MADE BY MANIPULATING A LONG STRIP OF FELTED FABRIC AND CAN BE EITHER MACHINE OR HAND STITCHED.

MATERIALS

- ♥ *13$^1/_2$ x 2 in. (34 x 5 cm) piece of pink felted knitting or felt for the rose*
- ♥ *small pieces of felted knitting or felt in green and aqua*
- ♥ *polyester sewing threads in matching colors*
- ♥ *fine hand embroidery or rayon machine embroidery threads in toning colors*
- ♥ *hair elastic, barrette, pin back, or length of suede ribbon for choker*

EQUIPMENT

- ♥ *cardstock, pencil, and ruler to make templates*
- ♥ *scissors—paper, fabric, and embroidery*
- ♥ *flat flower or glass-headed pins*
- ♥ *sewing needle*
- ♥ *thimble*
- ♥ *sewing machine (optional)*

1

2

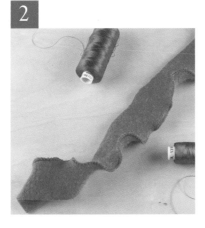

3

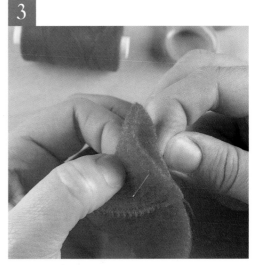

1 Draw a 13¹/₂ x 2 in. (34 x 5 cm) rectangle onto cardstock. Draw a line from one corner to halfway along the opposite short edge of the rectangle so that you have a strip that has one end narrower than the other. Cut out the template. Draw a leaf shape about 3¹/₂ in. (9 cm) long and 2 in. (5 cm) wide and cut out. Pin the templates onto the felt and cut out one long pink strip and one green leaf.

2 Using two toning colors of rayon embroidery thread, one as the top thread and one in the bobbin, machine sew along one edge of the strip of felt using satin stitch. This will make the edge slightly wavy. If you would like to hand stitch, work along the edge using buttonhole stitch and hand embroidery thread. This technique will not give a wavy edge but a satisfying homespun look.

Using embroidery thread in the loopers of a serger is a pretty way to decorate the wavy edges of your rose

3 Thread a needle with a doubled length of matching sewing thread. Starting at the widest end of the strip, fold the corner down to meet the bottom (unsewn) edge and stitch in place.

4 Roll the strip tightly for the first 6 in. (15 cm) and stitch

firmly in place at the bottom edge, pushing the needle through the whole roll of fabric. Turn the strip over and roll it in the opposite direction. This will form an "S" shape in the rose. Stitch firmly in place at the bottom edge.

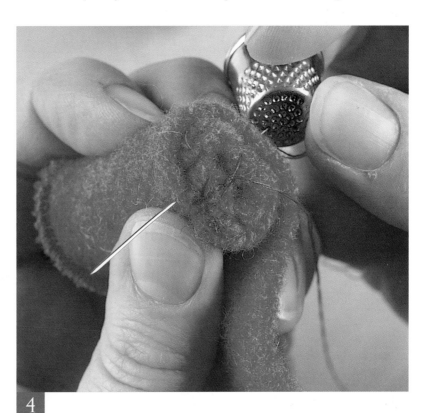

4

5

6

7

5 Start to loop out the edge of the felt slightly as you roll, making a firm stitch every ¾ in. (2 cm) to secure each loop. Continue in this way until only 1½ in. (3 cm) of the strip is left. Fold down the remaining top corner to the bottom edge and stitch in place as before.

6 Work around the bottom of rose with more stitching, pulling in loops as you go. Finish off with some firm back stitches.

7 Pin the leaf onto the piece of aqua felt. Change the embroidery threads in the machine to two shades of green. Embroider veins on the leaf using straight stitch, attaching the leaf to the background fabric at the same time. Satin stitch around the edge using a different shade of green as the top thread, then cut out the leaf, being careful not to cut through the stitching. (The four stages of making the leaf are shown here for clarity; you only need to make one leaf.) If you are hand stitching, first embroider the leaf veins using stab and back stitch in a different shade of green. Cut out

the second leaf shape and blanket stitch the two pieces together using green hand embroidery thread.

MAKING UP

8 Sew the leaf to the bottom of the rose using matching sewing

thread. Sew the base of the leaf to a hair elastic, barrette, pin back, or length of suede ribbon. If you are making a barrette, you may need to make two leaves in a slightly larger size in order to cover the barrette. Trim any loose ends of thread.

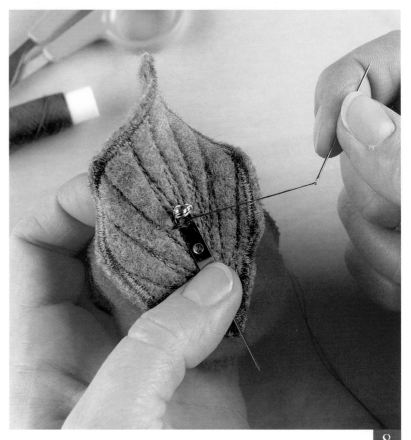

8

daisy barrette

HOW LONG?

embroidery and construction: **1 ho**

SMALL MOTIFS ARE EASY TO MAKE FROM SCRAPS OF FELT LEFT OVER FROM OTHER PROJECTS, THEN USED TO CREATE SMALL ACCESSORIES. THIS DAISY HAS BEEN MADE INTO A BARRETTE, BUT YOU COULD ALSO MAKE A PIN OR OTHER PIECE OF JEWELRY USING THIS DESIGN.

MATERIALS

- ♥ *small pieces of felted knitting or felt in red, pink, and orange*
- ♥ *6 x 6 in. (15 x 15 cm) piece of pink felted knitting or felt for backing*
- ♥ *polyester sewing threads in matching colors*
- ♥ *rayon machine embroidery threads in pink, red, and yellow*
- ♥ *3 in. (7.5 cm) long barrette*

EQUIPMENT

- ♥ *cardstock and pencil to make templates*
- ♥ *scissors—paper and embroidery*
- ♥ *flat flower or glass-headed pins*
- ♥ *sewing needle*
- ♥ *thimble*
- ♥ *sewing machine*

Use different motifs, such as flowers and butterflies, to create a range of jewelry or decorative patches for clothes

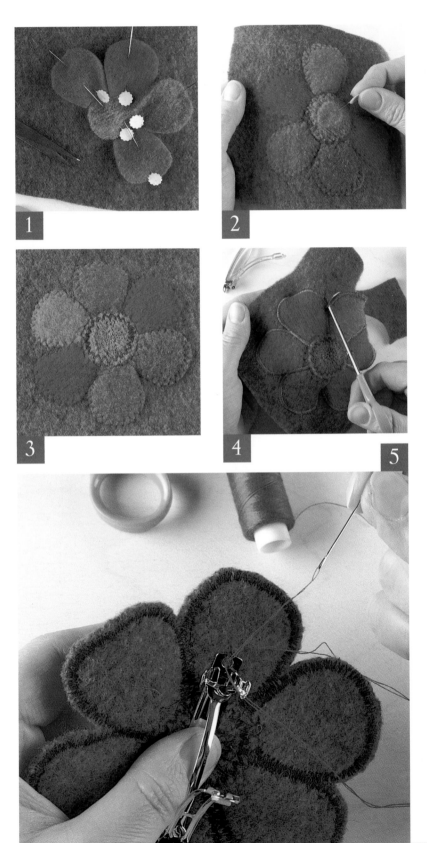

1 Trace the template on page 120 and cut out all the parts. Pin them onto small pieces of felt and cut out six petals of varying colors and one center circle. Pin the pieces in a daisy design on the backing felt. Machine sew in place using zigzag stitch and matching sewing threads.

2 Cut out a smaller circle in a different color from the first one, then pin and stitch this in the center of the daisy as before.

3 Leaving the matching sewing thread in the bobbin, use yellow embroidery thread as the top thread to sew a star inside the small circle using straight stitch. Change to red embroidery thread and select a machine stitch to embellish the larger circle. A wavy line is used here, but you could use a scallop stitch instead.

4 Outline the flower petals with satin stitch using pink embroidery thread. Carefully cut out the daisy with embroidery scissors, taking care not to cut through the satin stitching.

MAKING UP

5 Trim any loose ends of thread and press the daisy flat. Sew a barrette onto the reverse of the daisy using matching sewing thread.

HOW LONG?
embroidery and construction
1 hour

pom-pom hair band

THIS IS ANOTHER QUICK AND SIMPLE PROJECT THAT LOOKS GREAT. THE POM-POMS ARE HAND EMBROIDERED AND PADDED WITH POLYESTER BATTING. THEY ARE MADE IN SUBTLE TONES OF MAUVE AND WHITE, AND FEATURE VINTAGE MOTHER-OF-PEARL BUTTONS FROM A THRIFT STORE. EXPLORE OTHER COLOR SCHEMES USING BRIGHTER FELTS AND CONTRASTING BUTTONS FOR A DIFFERENT LOOK.

MATERIALS

♥ *4 x 4 in. (10 x 10 cm) piece of mauve felted knitting or felt*
♥ *two small mother-of-pearl buttons*
♥ *white rayon embroidery thread*
♥ *small amount of polyester batting*
♥ *elastic hair band*

EQUIPMENT

♥ *cardstock, pencil, ruler, and compass to make templates*
♥ *scissors—paper, fabric, and embroidery*
♥ *flat flower or glass-headed pins*
♥ *embroidery needle*
♥ *thimble*

Make different colored pom-poms to tone with your clothes

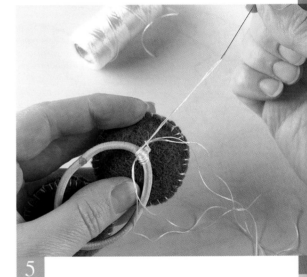

1 Draw a 2 in. (5 cm) diameter circle onto cardstock and cut out. Pin the template onto the felt and cut out four circles, two for the front and two for the back of the pom-poms.

2 Sew a button onto the center of two of the felt circles using a doubled strand of rayon embroidery thread. Decorate around one of the buttons using lazy daisy stitches, then add stab stitches in between. Decorate around the other button with cross stitches.

MAKING UP

3 Pin each decorated circle onto a plain one, wrong sides together. Work around each pair of felt circles with buttonhole stitch, leaving a 1¹/₄ in. (3 cm) gap.

4 Stuff the pom-poms with polyester batting. Use a pencil or the end of a knitting needle to help push the batting in. Sew the gap closed using buttonhole stitch.

5 Sew a pom-pom to opposite ends of the hair elastic using firm stitches and doubled embroidery thread.

love-heart pin

HOW LONG?
embroidery and construction: **1 hour**

HEARTS HAVE ALWAYS BEEN A GREAT FAVORITE OF MINE, AND SMALL ITEMS LIKE THIS PIN ARE VERY QUICK AND SATISFYING TO MAKE WITH MINIMAL EQUIPMENT. THE PIN FEATURES HAND EMBROIDERY AND IS PADDED WITH POLYESTER BATTING TO MAKE A FUN ITEM TO BRIGHTEN UP A JACKET LAPEL.

MATERIALS
- ♥ $3^1/2$ x $3^1/2$ in. (9 x 9 cm) piece of pink felted knitting or felt
- ♥ $3^1/2$ x 6 in. (9 x 15 cm) piece of red felted knitting or felt
- ♥ small green button
- ♥ rayon embroidery threads in orange, red, pink, and green (six-stranded green thread is used here)
- ♥ polyester sewing thread in matching colors
- ♥ small amount of polyester batting
- ♥ $1^1/4$ in. (3 cm) long pin back

EQUIPMENT
- ♥ cardstock, pencil, ruler, and compass to make patterns and templates
- ♥ scissors—paper, fabric, and embroidery
- ♥ flat flower or glass-headed pins
- ♥ embroidery needle
- ♥ sewing needle
- ♥ thimble
- ♥ hand embroidery and sewing needles

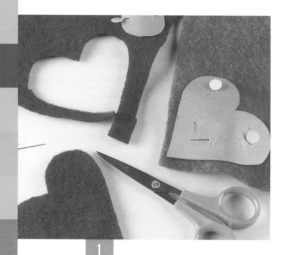

1

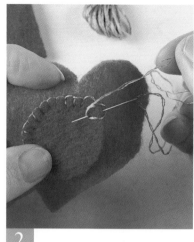

2

3

1 Use the heart template from page 120 and draw a 1¹/₂ in. (4 cm) diameter circle. Cut out both templates. Pinning the templates to the felt, cut out a pink heart for the front of the pin, a red heart for the back of the pin, and one red circle.

2 Pin the circle to the center of the pink heart and hand sew in place using two strands of green rayon embroidery thread and buttonhole stitch.

3 Sew a button to the center of the circle using green embroidery thread.

4 Using doubled strands of embroidery thread, decorate around the button, alternating orange lazy daisy stitches with pink stab stitches.

4

5 Stitch stars in the upper corners and base of the heart using two strands of green embroidery thread. Fill in the spaces with cross stitch and French knots using doubled strands of red and orange embroidery threads.

MAKING UP

6 Pin the two hearts wrong sides together and sew around the edges using buttonhole stitch and two strands of green embroidery thread, leaving a 1¹⁄₂ in. (4 cm) gap along one side.

7 Stuff the heart with polyester batting, ensuring that the heart is evenly padded. Use the end of a knitting needle or pencil to poke batting into the corners. Stitch up the heart with buttonhole stitch.

8 Sew a pin back to the back of the heart using matching polyester sewing thread.

5

6

7

8

bubble scarf and bag

HOW LONG?
embroidery: **1 day** (scarf); **3 hours** (bag
construction: **2 hours** (bag)

KNITTING RETAINS ITS KNITTED STRUCTURE AFTER FELTING AND REMAINS SLIGHTLY STRETCHY, SO IT CAN BE MANIPULATED INTO A BUBBLE TEXTURE USING FREE-MOTION MACHINE EMBROIDERY. THIS IS LESS SUCCESSFUL WITH OTHER TYPES OF FELT, BUT TRY OUT A FEW KINDS TO JUDGE THE EFFECT. THIS PROJECT USES A MACHINE KNITTED SCARF (SEE PAGE 12), BUT YOU COULD RECYCLE A SCARF. THICKER EMBROIDERY THREADS THAN USUAL ARE USED, SO MAKE A SAMPLE TO PRACTICE THE TECHNIQUE BEFORE STARTING WORK.

MATERIALS
♥ *60 x 12 in. (150 x 30 cm) piece of felted knitting*
♥ *standard rayon embroidery thread in a toning color*
♥ *thick rayon embroidery threads in four toning colors (for use on a bobbin)*

EQUIPMENT
♥ *embroidery scissors*
♥ *sewing machine with free-motion embroidery function*
♥ *steam iron and pressing cloth*

By using circular stitching with free-motion embroidery, you can produce this bubbly texture

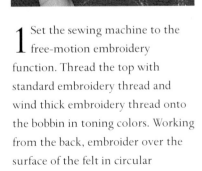

motions. Construct a series of randomly sized circles, taking care not to work in the centers. The stitches will draw in the felt, leaving the centers raised.

2 Change the bobbin thread to a different color and go over the surface again with circular free machining. Repeat with the remaining two colors until the stitches are quite dense and the bubble effect is apparent. Trim off any loose ends of thread.

3 Using a steam iron and pressing cloth, apply steam to the scarf a small section at a time. While it is still warm and damp, push your fingers into each bubble to manipulate the felt still further.

1 Set the sewing machine to the free-motion embroidery function. Thread the top with standard embroidery thread and wind thick embroidery thread onto the bobbin in toning colors. Working from the back, embroider over the surface of the felt in circular

bubble bag

THIS BAG IN CANDY COLORS USES THE SAME FREE-MOTION EMBROIDERY TECHNIQUE AS THE BUBBLE SCARF. THE CONFECTIONERY FEEL IS FURTHER EMPHASIZED BY THE PINK HANDLES. CLEAR PLASTIC BAG HANDLES CAN BE DYED AT HOME USING COMMERCIAL MULTIPURPOSE DYE AND ADD A STYLISH FINISH TO THE BAG.

Move on to this candy colored bag with dyed-to-match handles

1 Baste a diagonal line of stitches across the bottom corners of each piece of felt (the longer edges will be the top and bottom of the bag). Set the machine to the free-motion embroidery function. Thread the top with green polyester sewing thread and wind embroidery thread onto the bobbin. Embroider the felt to create a bubble fabric, using each color of thread, then steam and manipulate the bubbles by hand.

Take care not to embroider inside the marked corners or in the seam allowance of ³/₄ in. (1.5 cm). Trim off any loose ends of thread.

MAKING UP

2 Place the felt pieces right sides together and pin along the sides and base of the bag. Machine sew all three seams using straight stitch and green sewing thread. Trim the seams to ¹/₄ in. (5 mm).

3 Make box corners by folding and matching the side seam to the base seam in each bottom corner. Pin at 45 degrees, 1¹/₂ in. (3 cm) in from the corner. Stitch across with straight stitch and trim back to ¹/₄ in. (5 mm). Turn the bag right side out and press the seams and corners carefully, taking care to retain the shape of the bubbles; firmly push them out with your fingers again if necessary. Press and baste a ³/₄ in. (1.5 cm) hem around the top edge of the bag.

MATERIALS
♥ *two 10 x 12 in. (25 x 30 cm) pieces of green felted knitting*
♥ *green and pink polyester sewing thread*
♥ *thick rayon embroidery thread in five toning colors (for use on a bobbin)*
♥ *basting thread in a contrasting color*
♥ *two 10 x 12 in. (25 x 30 cm) pieces of pink silk for lining*
♥ *two clear plastic handles*
♥ *red or pink hot water dye*

EQUIPMENT
♥ *embroidery scissors*
♥ *flat flower or glass-headed pins*
♥ *sewing needle*
♥ *thimble*
♥ *sewing machine with free-motion embroidery function*
♥ *steam iron and pressing cloth*

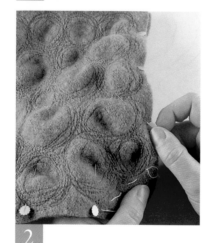

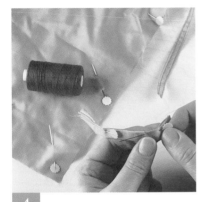

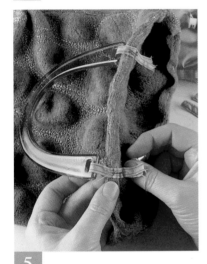

4 Pin the pieces of silk right sides together and stitch around the sides and base using pink sewing thread. Create box corners as for the felt section. Fold and press a $^3/_4$ in. (1.5 cm) hem around the top edge. Cut four $4^1/_2$ x $1^1/_2$ in. (11.5 x 4 cm) strips of silk that include a selvage. Fold each strip in three lengthwise so that the selvage is outermost and pin in place. Machine stitch down each side of the strips using straight stitch and pink sewing thread.

5 Dye the handles according to manufacturer's instructions. If you want pastel-colored handles, check the color regularly to make sure it is not too deep. Mark the position of the handles on the inside of the felt bag, ensuring they are symmetrical and the handles will meet. Thread a strip of silk through each of the slots on the handles and hand stitch the strip to the hem on the top edge of the felt bag using green sewing thread.

6 Place the lining inside the bag wrong sides together. Match the seams, then pin and baste the lining in place so that the top edge of the felt is slightly raised above the lining.

7 Machine sew two parallel rows of straight stitching around the top edge of the bag in pink with green on the bobbin. It is easiest to work with the silk lining uppermost. The two rows of stitching ensure that the handles are secure in the seam. Trim off any ends of thread.

earflap hat

HOW LONG?
embroidery: **2–3 evenings**
construction: $^1/_2$ **hour**

THIS BABY'S HAT HAS EARFLAPS CUT AS PART OF THE MAIN SHAPE AND IS EASY TO CONSTRUCT. IT FEATURES CIRCLES DECORATED WITH HAND EMBROIDERY AND BUTTONS TO FORM FLOWERS. THE PATTERN IS DESIGNED TO FIT AN 18 IN. (46 CM) HEAD CIRCUMFERENCE, SO YOU MAY NEED TO ADJUST THE HAT TO FIT YOUR BABY.

MATERIALS
♥ 22 x 12 in. (55 x 30 cm) piece of mauve felted knitting
♥ small pieces of felted knitting in shades of pink, orange, and green
♥ eight small buttons in toning colors
♥ mauve polyester sewing thread
♥ fine wool embroidery thread in toning colors

EQUIPMENT
♥ cardstock, pencil, ruler, and compass to make patterns and templates
♥ scissors—paper, fabric, and embroidery
♥ masking tape (if you need to adjust size of pattern)
♥ flat flower or glass-headed pins
♥ embroidery needle
♥ thimble
♥ sewing machine or serger
♥ steam iron and pressing cloth

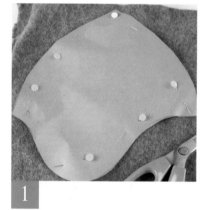

1

2

1 Enlarge the pattern on page 120 on a photocopier. Measure the baby's head, divide this figure by two, and adjust the pattern along the indicated lines if necessary. Fix alterations in place with strips of masking tape. Add a $^1/_4$ in. (0.5 cm) seam allowance around the top seam. Fold the mauve felt in half widthwise, pin the pattern onto it, and cut out two pieces.

2 Draw $3^1/_2$, 2, and $1^3/_4$ in. (9, 5, and 4.5 cm) diameter circles onto cardstock and cut out. Draw and cut out a $2^1/_2$ in. (6 cm) long leaf shape. Pin the templates to the felt and cut out four small and two medium circles in different colors; distribute them in the top area of both hat pieces in a symmetrical design. Cut out four green leaves and pin them between the circles. Cut out two large pink circles and pin them to the earflaps. Cut out two small orange circles and pin them inside the large circles.

*Make this hat in
lambswool for a softer feel*

3

4

5

3 Hand appliqué the circles and leaves onto the hat using doubled strands of contrasting colored embroidery threads and buttonhole stitch. Embroider veins on the leaves using back stitch and stab stitch.

4 Sew buttons in the center of each circle using double strands of embroidery thread.

5 Decorate each circle with alternate lazy daisy and stab stitches using two different colored threads. Decorate the inner circle on the earflaps with running stitch.

6 Stitch stars in the remaining areas using yellow embroidery thread.

MAKING UP

7 Select a stretch stitch such as double overlock or zigzag, or use a serger, to sew the hat pieces together. Pin the hat pieces right sides together and sew the top seam using matching sewing thread.

8 Finish the open edge of the hat using two colors of embroidery thread in the loopers of the serger or hand finish with buttonhole stitch. Turn the hat right side out, trim off any loose ends of thread, and press carefully, rolling out the seams with your fingers.

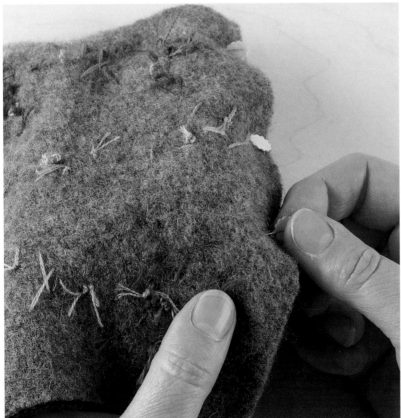

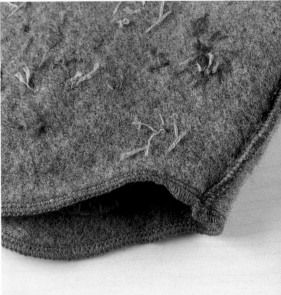

children's mittens

HOW LONG?
embroidery: **2 evenings**
construction: **1 hour**

THE SELECTION OF COLORS, HAND EMBROIDERY STITCHES, AND THE FLOWER BUTTONS GIVE THESE MITTENS A NAIVE CHARM. LOOK AT THE ADULT MITTEN PATTERN FOR IDEAS ON RECYCLING KNITWEAR FOR THIS PROJECT (SEE PAGE 54). WHEN MAKING ANY PROJECT FOR A YOUNG CHILD, MAKE SURE YOU SEW THE BUTTONS ON VERY SECURELY. THE MITTENS ARE ALSO ATTACHED TO A CORD SO THAT THEY WILL NOT BE LOST WHEN TAKEN OFF.

MATERIALS

♥ *12 x 16 in. (30 x 40 cm) piece of aqua blue felted knitting, depending on size of mittens*
♥ *small pieces of felted knitting in blue, pink, orange, and mauve*
♥ *18 small buttons in toning colors*
♥ *aqua blue polyester sewing thread*
♥ *rayon embroidery thread in toning colors*
♥ *40-60 in. (100-150 cm) length of orange rayon cord*

EQUIPMENT

♥ *cardstock, pencil, ruler, and compass to make patterns and templates*
♥ *scissors—paper, fabric, and embroidery*
♥ *flat flower or glass-headed pins*
♥ *embroidery needle*
♥ *thimble*
♥ *sewing machine*
♥ *steam iron and pressing cloth*

1

1 Place the child's hand onto a piece of cardstock with fingers together and thumb slightly apart. Draw around the hand and 2 in. (5 cm) down below the wrist. Round off the top of the finger and thumb sections to get a good basic mitten shape. Make sure the opening at the wrist is ¹/₂ in. (1 cm) wider than the wrist to allow the hand to get through. Add a ¹/₂ in. (1 cm) seam allowance all around, then cut out the pattern. Fold the aqua blue felt in half widthwise. Pin the pattern onto the fabric and cut out. Repeat for the second mitten. Make sure you have a top and an underside for each hand, with the right side of the fabric outermost, if discernible.

Lengths of shiny rayon cord help ensure the mittens don't get lost!

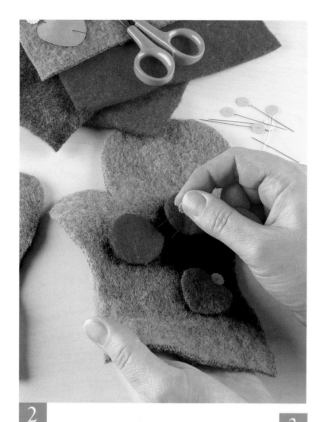

2

3

4

2 Make a 1¹/₂ in. (4 cm) diameter circle template and cut out eight small circles from the remaining colors of felt. Arrange four circles onto the top piece of each mitten and pin in place.

3 Using a doubled strand of contrasting colored embroidery thread, appliqué each circle in place using buttonhole stitch. Sew a button securely to the center of each circle and five others in the surrounding area on both mittens.

4 Decorate each circle with stab stitch in a contrasting color, then fill in the remaining spaces with star stitch.

MAKING UP

5 Pin each pair of mitten pieces right sides together. Using matching sewing thread, machine sew around the mitten using straight stitch and a $1/2$ in. (1 cm) seam allowance. Trim the seam to $1/4$ in. (5 mm) all around.

6 Turn the mittens right side out, using a knitting needle or pencil to turn the thumb out. Roll out the seams using your fingers.

7 Turn the seam allowance under around the wrist opening and machine sew in place using a stretch stitch, such as double overlock or zigzag, and matching sewing thread. Decorate the wrist opening using buttonhole stitch in a contrasting color. Press the mittens and ease them into shape. Measure the child from wrist to shoulder, across the back, and then from other shoulder to wrist. Cut the rayon cord to this length. Tie a knot at each end and stitch the cord to the inside seam (thumb side) of each mitten above the knot.

butterfly baby coat

THIS COAT IS DECORATED WITH FLOWERS AND BUTTERFLIES, THEIR FLIGHT PATHS INDICATED BY LOOPS OF BACKSTITCH, BUT YOU COULD EASILY THEME THE DECORATION TO SUIT THE CHILD. THE PATTERN PROVIDED IS DESIGNED TO FIT A BABY OF AROUND SIX MONTHS, BUT YOU CAN EASILY ADJUST THE SIZE BY CUTTING ALONG THE LINES INDICATED AND MOVING THE PATTERN CLOSER OR FARTHER APART UNTIL THE CORRECT SIZE IS ACHIEVED. IT IS ALWAYS WORTH MAKING THE COAT A LITTLE BIGGER THAN NECESSARY BECAUSE BABIES GROW SO QUICKLY. MAKE SURE THE BUTTONS ARE STITCHED ON VERY FIRMLY FOR SAFETY.

MATERIALS

- ♥ *32 x 26 in. (80 x 65 cm) piece of dark green felted knitting, depending on size of coat*
- ♥ *small amounts of felted knitting in shades of pink and red*
- ♥ *polyester sewing thread in matching colors*
- ♥ *hand and machine rayon embroidery thread in toning colors*
- ♥ *basting thread in a contrasting color*
- ♥ *three or four ³/₄ in. (2 cm) diameter pink buttons*
- ♥ *10 x 2¹/₂ in. (25 x 6 cm) piece of tear away interlining*

EQUIPMENT

- ♥ *cardstock, pencil, and ruler to make patterns and templates*
- ♥ *scissors—paper, fabric, and embroidery*
- ♥ *masking tape (if you need to adjust size of pattern)*
- ♥ *flat flower or glass-headed pins*
- ♥ *embroidery needle*
- ♥ *sewing needle*
- ♥ *thimble*
- ♥ *sewing machine*
- ♥ *serger (optional)*
- ♥ *steam iron and pressing cloth*

*Adjust the theme and colors
of the coat to suit your child*

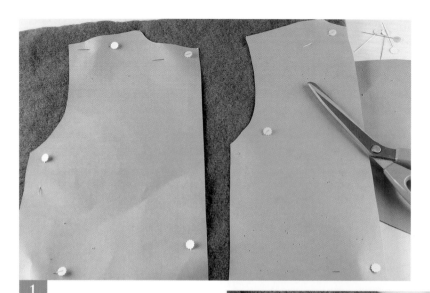

1

small butterflies. Arrange and pin the pieces onto the coat, spacing the butterflies evenly and facing in different directions.

3 Machine appliqué the butterflies in place using matching sewing thread and zigzag stitch. Cut out small circles of pink and red felt to fit inside the butterfly wings. Pin and stitch them in place in the same way.

1 Enlarge the patterns on pages 121–122 on a photocopier, adjusting the size if necessary along the lines indicated. Fix alterations in place with masking tape. Allow a $1/4$ in. (5 mm) allowance around the seams. On the edges that will be hemmed (neck, front, base, and base of sleeves) allow $3/4$ in. (1.5 cm). Allow an extra 1 in. (2.5 cm) at the center front of the pattern for the overlap where the jacket fastens. Fold the felt in half and pin the patterns onto it, making sure the center of the back pattern is placed on the fold. Cut out the pieces. You will have two sleeves, two fronts, and a complete back when opened out.

2 Trace the butterfly templates on page 121 onto cardstock. Cut out enough pieces of pink and red felt to compose six large butterflies and five

2

3

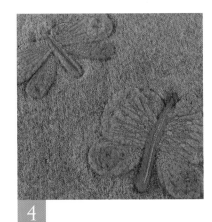

4

6

5

4 Machine embroider straight stitches to indicate veins on the wings using a toning color of embroidery thread. Add detail across the wings and inside the circles using satin stitch dots. Sew a line of wide satin stitch down the center of each butterfly's body. Use a narrow and then wide satin stitch to form antennae.

5 Hand embroider the looping flight paths of the butterflies using back stitch with pale green embroidery thread. Finish each trail with a few running stitches.

6 Hand embroider flowers between the butterflies using lazy daisy stitch and then stab stitch using tones of pink and red thread. Scatter star stitches across the remaining areas.

MAKING UP

7 Press all of the pieces, then place the fronts and back right sides together and pin the shoulders. Select a stretch stitch such as double overlock or zigzag, or use a serger, to sew the shoulder seams with matching sewing thread. Sew them edge to edge as the seam allowance is only ¹/₄ in. (5 mm)

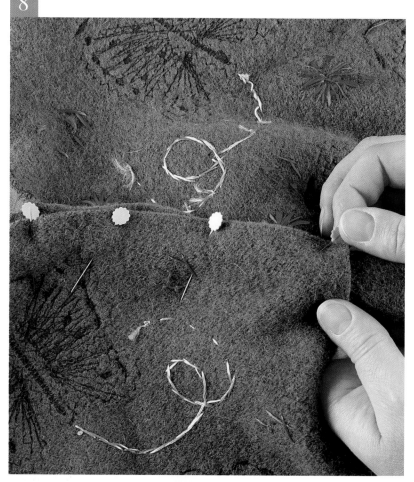

8 With right sides facing, fit the curved edge of the sleeves into the sleeve holes and pin. Stitch as before.

9 With right sides facing, pin and stitch the side and sleeve seams as before. Turn the jacket right side out and press the seams carefully.

10 Turn in and press ³/₄ in. (1.5 cm) hems on the ends of the sleeves, around the neck, down the front, and along the bottom of the jacket. Pin and baste, then machine sew with straight stitch. Decorate all the hems with buttonhole stitch using pink hand embroidery thread.

11 Baste tear away interlining onto the back of the right-hand side of the center opening. This will allow you to make buttonholes in the felt without stretching the fabric too much. Machine sew three or four evenly spaced buttonholes along the edge using matching sewing thread. Slit the buttonholes using embroidery scissors, tear away the interlining, and remove the basting stitches. Remove any remaining interlining with tweezers if necessary. Alternatively, cut small slits and work buttonholes by hand using buttonhole stitch and embroidery thread.

12 Mark the button positions on the left-hand of the center opening and sew the buttons in place with very firm stitching. Trim any loose ends of thread.

cosmic baby blanket

HOW LONG?

embroidery: **2–3 evenings**

construction: **4 hours**

MATERIALS
- ♥ *pieces of felted knitting in shades of blue and purple (see step 1 for dimensions)*
- ♥ *small pieces of felted knitting in shades of orange and yellow*
- ♥ *polyester sewing threads in matching colors*
- ♥ *rayon embroidery threads in toning colors*
- ♥ *basting thread in a contrasting color*

EQUIPMENT
- ♥ *cardstock, pencil, ruler, and compass to make patterns and templates*
- ♥ *scissors—paper, fabric, and embroidery*
- ♥ *flat flower or glass-headed pins*
- ♥ *embroidery needle*
- ♥ *sewing needle*
- ♥ *thimble*
- ♥ *sewing machine with free-motion embroidery function*
- ♥ *serger (optional)*
- ♥ *steam iron and pressing cloth*

THIS BLANKET WILL KEEP A YOUNG BABY WARM FOR OUTINGS IN CHILLY WEATHER. THE BLANKET MEASURES 28 X 32 IN. (70 X 80 CM), BUT IT IS EASY TO ADJUST THE SIZE; JUST REMEMBER TO ADD SEAM AND HEM ALLOWANCES ONTO EACH PIECE. IF YOU HAVE THE TIME AND MATERIALS, WHY NOT MAKE A LARGER THROW OR BLANKET? IT WOULD LOOK PARTICULARLY GOOD PATCHWORKED FROM RECYCLED SWEATERS. REFER TO THE DIAGRAM ON PAGE 123 WHEN MAKING UP THE BLANKET.

1 Cut out the background pieces in various shades of blue and purple. The dimensions given here include seam and hem allowances of ¹/₂ in. (1.5 cm).

PIECE A: 7 x 9 in. (18 x 23 cm)
PIECE B: 7 x 21 in. (18 x 53 cm)
PIECE C: 19 x 19 in. (48 x 48 cm)
PIECE D: 19 x 11 in. (48 x 28 cm)
PIECE E: 9 x 29 in. (23 x 76 cm)

The space theme could be used to great effect on the baby coat on page 94

2 Lay out the rectangles on a table top as indicated in the diagram and retain this layout throughout so that you can evaluate the design at all stages. Take care not to place motifs near the seam and hem allowances. Make templates as necessary from cardstock.

PIECE A: Cut out a 3 in. (8 cm) diameter circle of dark orange felt and pin it to the center of the piece. Alternate small triangles of light orange and yellow around the outside edge of the circle.

PIECE B: Cut four 3 in. (8 cm) diameter circles of dark orange felt and pin them in a crooked line along the piece.

PIECE C: Cut a 3 in. (8 cm) diameter circle of yellow felt and pin it off-center onto the piece. Cut out four triangles in dark oranges that are $4^1/2$ in. (11 cm) high. Cut out four triangles in light oranges that are $2^1/2$ in. (6 cm) high. All eight triangles should be 1 in. (2.5 cm) wide at the base. Pin the long triangles around the circle in the north, south, east, and west positions; pin the smaller triangles in

between. Make a star from four 7 x $^1/2$ in. (18 x 1 cm) strips of felt in oranges and yellows. Cut $3^1/2$, 3, and $2^1/2$ in. (9, 7.5, and 6 cm) diameter circles in various shades and pin them in the spaces around the two stars.

PIECE D: Cut two "S" shaped spirals from orange felt and pin on each side of the piece. Add an orange $2^1/2$ in. (8 cm) diameter circle in between.

PIECE E: Form four stars, each comprised of four 5 x $^1/2$ in. (12.5 x 1 cm) strips of felt in different colors, and pin them in a line across the piece.

Machine sew each motif in place using sewing thread and zigzag stitch. Use a color that matches the background fabric on the bobbin and a color that matches the motif as the top thread.

3 Cut smaller circles of felt in different shades and pin them in the center of each circle already sewn onto the background pieces. Zigzag in place.

4 Machine embroider details onto piece C. Use satin stitch to create bold lines along the rays of the larger star; use straight stitch to embroider rays on and around the smaller star; use satin stitch to create small dots among the rays.

5

6

7

5 Machine embroider the remaining pieces. Use straight stitch to embellish the rays of the stars on piece E and sew satin stitch dots in the surrounding area. Use free-motion embroidery to accent the spirals on piece D and some of the circles on the other pieces. Stitch stars in the remaining circles and surrounding areas. Press each piece.

MAKING UP

6 Pin pieces A and B right sides together, making sure the motifs are the right way up. Select a stretch stitch, such as double overlock or zigzag, or use a serger, to sew the seam. If using a serger, make sure the blade trims off the correct seam allowance. If using a sewing machine, trim the seams back to align with the stitching. Repeat with pieces C and D. Repeat to sew AB and CD together, then sew piece E along bottom edge of CD.

7 Press along each seam. Turn and press a $^1\!/_2$ in. (1 cm) hem around the edge of the blanket. Pin and baste into place. Machine sew using straight stitch and matching sewing thread, then hand embroider the edge with buttonhole stitch in a contrasting color embroidery thread. Trim any loose ends of thread.

heartwarming scarf

HOW LONG?
embroidery: **1 evening**
construction: **1–2 hours**

THIS FUNKY SCARF HAS POCKETS SEWN ON EACH END TO
GIVE CHILDREN A PLACE TO KEEP THEIR HANDS WARM.
HEARTWARMING TONES OF RED AND PINK ARE PERFECT FOR
THE SCARF AND APPLIQUÉD HEART MOTIFS. A LENGTH OF
FELTED KNITTING HAS BEEN USED HERE, BUT YOU COULD USE
RECYCLED PIECES PATCHED TOGETHER WITH A STRETCH STITCH
ON THE MACHINE, OR RECYCLE A COMPLETE SCARF YOU
ALREADY HAVE.

MATERIALS

- ♥ *8 x 55 in. (20 x 140 cm) piece of pink felted knitting or felt*
- ♥ *8 x 14 in. (20 x 36 cm) piece of red felted knitting or felt*
- ♥ *small pieces of felted knitting or felt in shades of pink*
- ♥ *polyester sewing thread in matching colors*
- ♥ *rayon embroidery thread in golden yellow and toning shades of pink*

EQUIPMENT

- ♥ *cardstock, pencil, ruler, and compass to make templates*
- ♥ *scissors—paper, fabric, and embroidery*
- ♥ *flat flower or glass-headed pins*
- ♥ *sewing machine*
- ♥ *serger or sewing needle*
- ♥ *steam iron and pressing cloth*

1

1 Round off the corners of the pink
felt using embroidery scissors, then
neaten all around the edge. If you have a
serger, thread pink and red embroidery
threads through the loopers and needles.
Otherwise, work around the edge by
hand using buttonhole stitch in either
color of thread.

There's no reason why the pocket idea cannot be used on a scarf for an adult

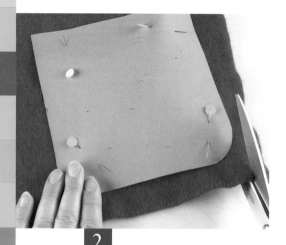

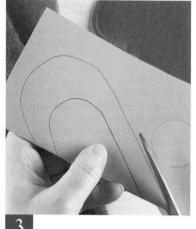

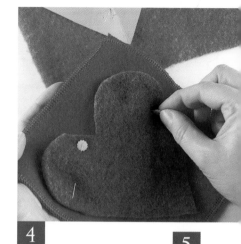

2

3

4

5

2 Draw a 7 x 7 ½ in. (18 x 19 cm) rectangle onto cardstock. Round off the bottom two corners (the shorter edges form the top and bottom of the pockets) and cut out. Pin the template onto red felt and cut out two pockets. Neaten the edges as before.

3 Fold a piece of cardstock in half and draw a half heart shape about 5½ in. (14 cm) high and 3 in. (7.5 cm) wide. Draw a smaller heart inside measuring 3½ in. (9 cm) high and 2½ in. (6 cm) wide. Draw a 1½ in. (4 cm) diameter circle in one corner and a 2 in. (5 cm) diameter circle on the other side of the folded cardstock. Cut out the larger heart and the two circles.

4 Cut large hearts in two shades of pink felt. Pin the hearts to the pockets and machine sew in place using zigzag stitch and matching sewing thread.

5 Cut out four small circles in shades of pink felt and pin them in the bottom corners of the pockets. Cut some larger circles of felt in shades of red and pink. Scatter them evenly up and down length of scarf and pin in place. Stitch as before. Cut down the heart template to the smaller size and cut two small hearts in different shades of pink. Pin and stitch them onto the larger hearts.

6
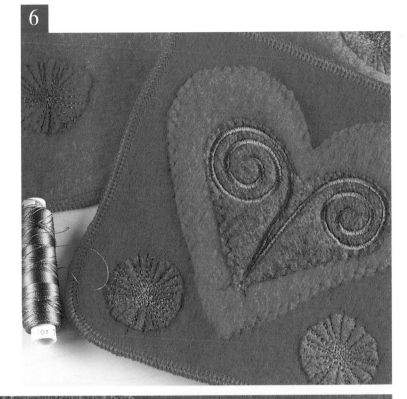

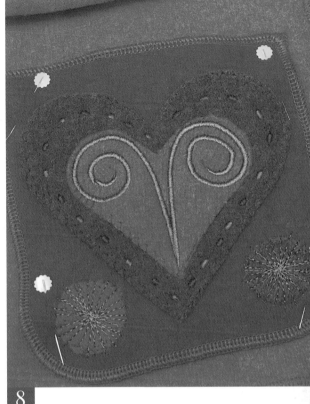
8

7
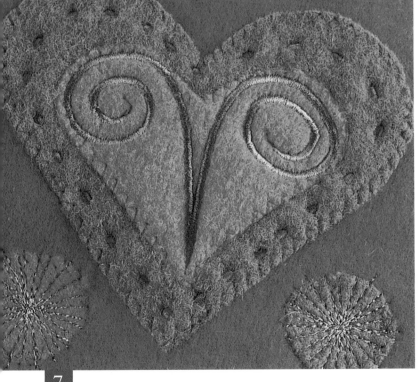

6 Using golden yellow embroidery thread, machine sew spirals of satin stitch inside the small hearts. Use the same thread to sew stars inside all the circles.

7 Decorate the larger hearts with satin stitch dots in red and pink embroidery thread.

MAKING UP
8 Pin the pockets in place at each end of the scarf, making sure there is equal space around the bottom three edges. Machine sew close to these three edges using straight stitch. Trim any loose ends of thread, then press the scarf.

bunny slippers

HOW LONG?
embroidery: **1 hour**
construction: **4–5 hours**

These endearing bunny slippers can easily be adapted to other favorite animals, such as dogs or kittens. Use a more substantial felt than normal—for example, wash knitted lambswool at 140° F (60°C) instead of the usual 90°F (30°C). You can also use recycled knitwear that has felted too thickly and is unsuitable for anything else. Before you embark on the real thing, make a test slipper to be sure the fit is correct.

MATERIALS

♥ 25 x 18 in. (64 x 46 cm) piece of extra-thick brown felted knitting, depending on size of slippers
♥ $6^{1}/2$ x $4^{1}/2$ in. (16.5 x 11.5 cm) piece of pinky brown felted knitting
♥ extra-strong polyester sewing thread in matching colors
♥ black embroidery thread
♥ four $^{5}/8$ in. (1.5 cm) diameter black buttons
♥ latex glue (optional)

EQUIPMENT

♥ cardstock, pencil and ruler to make patterns and templates
♥ scissors—paper, fabric, and embroidery
♥ flat flower or glass-headed pins
♥ embroidery needle
♥ thimble
♥ sewing machine
♥ steam iron and pressing cloth
♥ tissue paper and paintbrush (optional)

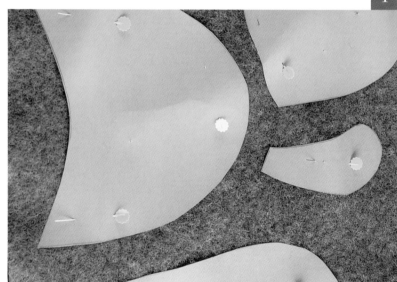

1

1 Enlarge the patterns on page 124 using a photocopier. You will have a sole, front, back, and an ear. Measure the length of the child's foot and adjust the sole pattern if necessary along the lines indicated. Fix alterations in place with masking tape and remember to allow a $^3/4$ in. (1.5 cm) seam allowance all around. Measure and adjust the width of the sole and the width of the upper front in the same way. Fold the extra-thick felt in half and pin the sole and front pattern pieces onto it. Cut out so that you have two of each piece. Repeat for the outer ears and slipper back; you need four of each. Cut four inner ears from pinky brown felt, making these slighty narrower than the outer ears.

By adjusting the pattern, you will be able to make the slippers fit most children

2 Using black embroidery thread, stitch crosses for a nose and use stab stitch to create whiskers either side of the face on both slipper front. Sew two buttons onto each to form eyes.

3 Pin a pinky brown inner ear on top of each outer ear. Check that you have the ears the right way up and that there are two right and two left ears. Machine stitch in place using zigzag stitch and matching thread.

4 Using black embroidery thread, work buttonhole stitch around the four outer ear pieces.

MAKING UP

5 Pin pairs of back pieces wrong sides together and machine sew the back seam using straight stitch and matching polyester sewing thread. Trim the seam back to 1/4 in. (5 mm).

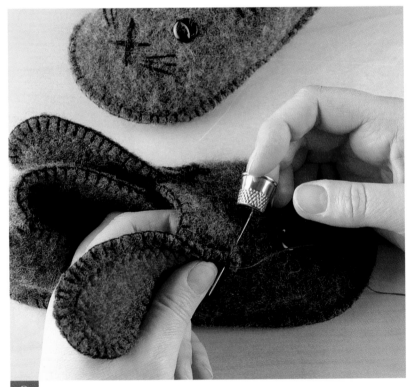

6 Decorate the back seam using black embroidery thread and buttonhole stitch. Also decorate the top edges (indicated on the pattern) of the front and back sections of each slipper.

7 With wrong sides together, fit and pin the backs of the slippers around the back section of the soles. Baste in place. Do the same with the fronts, making sure the center points of the fronts and sole align (marked on pattern). Note that the front pieces will overlap the back pieces at the sides. Baste in place. Machine sew using straight stitch and matching sewing thread. Trim the seam to $1/4$ in. (5 mm) and decorate it using black embroidery thread and buttonhole stitch.

8 Shape each ear by pinching it together at the base. Hand stitch them in place using matching sewing thread. To make a nonslip sole, fill the slippers with rolled tissue paper to keep their shape, then turn them over and paint the soles with latex glue. Allow to dry, then repeat this process two more times.

backpack with bird

HOW LONG?
embroidery: **1-2 evenings**
construction: **3 hours**

THIS BACKPACK IS DECORATED WITH A BRIGHT FOLK ART BIRD AND STARS. A CHUNKY TOGGLE FASTENING FINISHES THE BAG. MEASURE YOUR CHILD TO SEE HOW LONG TO MAKE THE STRAPS. IF YOU WANT TO MAKE THE STRAPS ADJUSTABLE, MAKE EACH STRAP IN TWO SECTIONS WITH BUTTONHOLES AND BUTTONS ALONG THE LENGTH.

MATERIALS

- ♥ 36 x 12 in. (90 x 30 cm) piece of dark blue felted knitting or felt
- ♥ 24 x 3 in. (60 x 7.5 cm) piece of pink felted knitting or felt
- ♥ small pieces of felted knitting or felt in shades of red, pink, and green
- ♥ polyester sewing threads in matching colors
- ♥ rayon embroidery threads in toning colors
- ♥ 48 in. (120 cm) length of 1 in. (2.5 cm) wide tape to strengthen straps
- ♥ 2 in. (5 cm) long toggle

EQUIPMENT

- ♥ cardstock, pencil, ruler, and compass to make patterns and templates
- ♥ scissors—paper, fabric, and embroidery
- ♥ flat flower or glass-headed pins
- ♥ sewing needle
- ♥ thimble
- ♥ sewing machine
- ♥ steam iron and pressing cloth

1

2

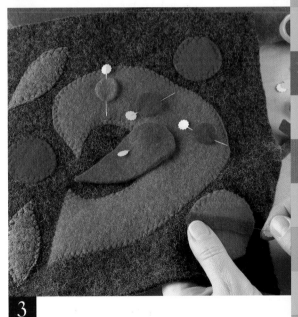

3

1 Enlarge the bag patterns on pages 125–126 on a photocopier and cut out. You should have a front, back, and flap. Pin the pattern pieces onto a single layer of dark blue felt and cut out.

2 Copy the bird and wing designs on page 126 and make templates. Cut out a bird from pink felt and a wing from red felt. Make templates of $2^1/2$ in. and $1^3/4$ in. (6 and 4.5 cm) diameter circles. Cut out two small and one large circle in shades of red and pink. Cut out two $3^1/4$ in. (8 cm) long leaves in different shades of green. Pin the bird, circles, and leaves onto the front flap of the bag, leaving a $3/4$ in. (2 cm) hem and seam allowance around the edge. Machine sew in place using zigzag stitch and matching sewing thread.

3 Pin the wing onto the bird. Cut out three small circles, about $3/4$ in. (2 cm) diameter, in various colors and pin them onto the bird. Pin three small strips of felt in varying shades onto the largest circle to form a star. Stitch all the pieces in place as before.

Make use of traditional folk art motifs in your designs

4 Decorate the motifs with machine embroidery using various shades of rayon embroidery thread. Sew satin stitch lines on the bird's tail and wing. Decorate the bird's breast and wing with dots of satin stitch. Use a dark color thread to form the bird's eye. Use straight stitch to add veins to the leaves and along the rays of the star. If you have a free-motion embroidery function on your sewing machine, embroider the very small circles with lines of circular stitching; otherwise use star stitch. Use star stitch to embroider the remaining spaces and circles.

5 Measure the child to determine how long to make the straps, then cut two 3 in. (7.5 cm) wide strips of the correct length in pink felt. Fold and pin the felt strips around the tape. Machine sew down the center using zigzag stitch and matching sewing thread.

MAKING UP

6 Pin the back and top edge of the flap right sides together with the ends of the straps inserted into the seam at the center. Pin the other ends of the straps to the bottom corners of the back piece. Make sure the ends of the straps extend slightly beyond the edge of the bag. Machine sew the top flap and back seam using matching sewing thread, making sure that the tops of the straps are also sewn in. Sew another row close to the first for extra strength. Trim the fabric close to the seam.

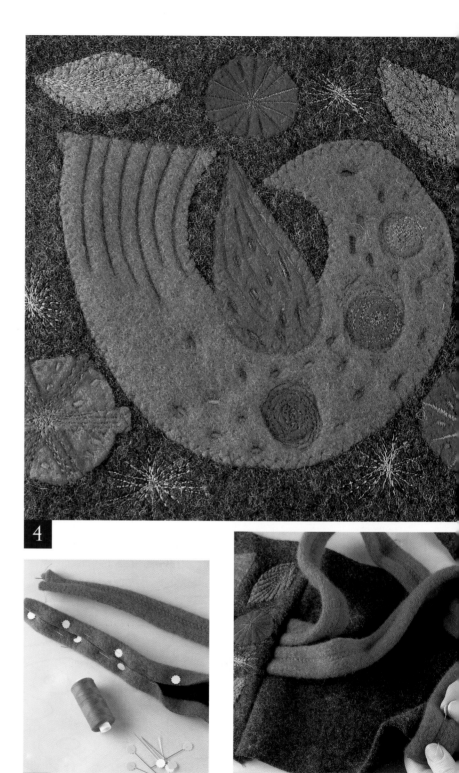

4

5

6

7 Place the front of the bag onto the back piece, right sides together, and covering the straps. Pin in place and stitch around the base and sides as before. Add another row of stitching for extra strength close to the first. Trim close to the seam.

8 Turn the bag right side out and press, rolling out the seams with your fingers to get a neat finish.

9 Turn under and press a $^1/_2$ in. (1 cm) hem around the edge of the flap and the top front edge of the bag. Pin and baste in place. Machine sew using straight stitch and matching sewing thread.

10 Cut a 4 in. (10 cm) length of pink felt; the rolled edge from a piece of machine knitting has been used here, but you could cut a wider strip, fold it and sew down the center. Fold the strip in half to form a loop and stitch the ends together, then sew it to the bottom center edge of the flap. Determine the position of the toggle and stitch in place. Trim any loose ends of thread.

patterns

ENLARGE THE PATTERNS ON A PHOTOCOPIER BY THE PERCENTAGE GIVEN. NOT ALL OF THEM WILL FIT ON STANDARD SIZED PAPER, SO COPY THEM IN SEVERAL PARTS, CUT OUT THE PIECES, AND TAPE THEM TOGETHER WITH MASKING TAPE. MAKE ANY NECESSARY SIZE ADJUSTMENTS, USING TAPE TO HOLD THE PATTERNS IN PLACE. TRANSFER THE CORRECT SIZED PATTERN ONTO CARDSTOCK, FIXING IT IN PLACE WITH TAPE BEFORE CUTTING AROUND EACH PIECE. THIS WILL MAKE A LONG-LASTING PATTERN YOU CAN USE AGAIN AND AGAIN.

russian hat

PAGE 28

Cut on fold

SIDE

CUT 1
(Enlarge by 200%)

CROWN

CUT 1
(Enlarge by 160%)

CUFF
CUT 1
(Enlarge by 160%)

Cut on fold

starburst handbag

PAGE 44

HANDLE

CUT 2
(Enlarge by 160%)

FRONT AND BACK

CUT 2
(Enlarge by 160%)

TOP CUFF

CUT 1
(Enlarge by 160%)

Cut on fold

tote bag

PAGE 50

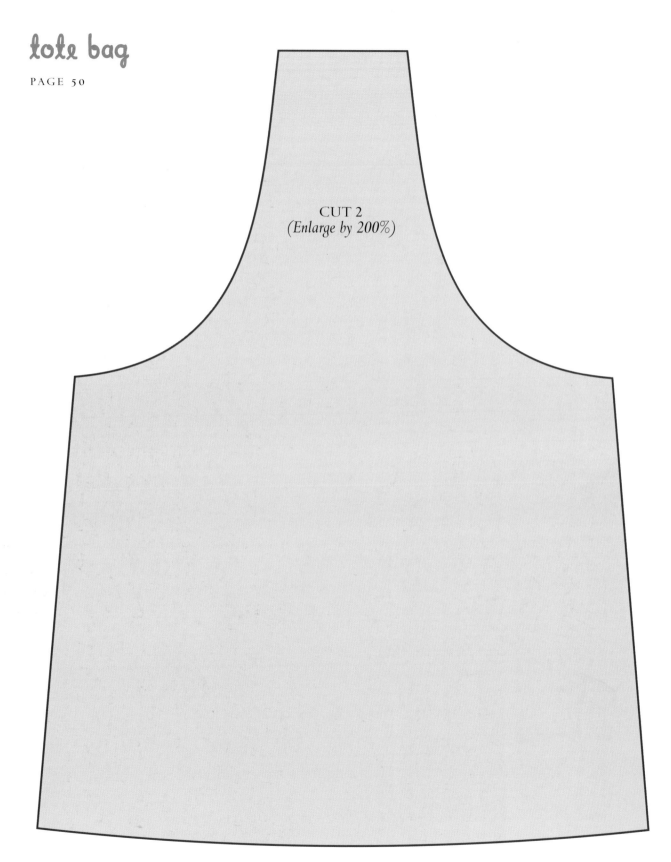

CUT 2
(Enlarge by 200%)

oriental slippers

PAGE 58

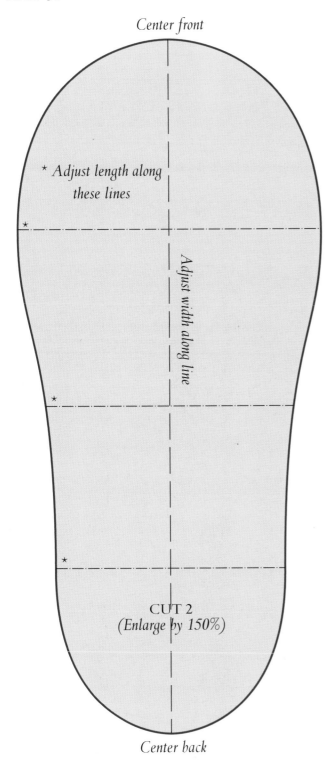

Center front

★ *Adjust length along these lines*

Adjust width along line

CUT 2
(Enlarge by 150%)

Center back

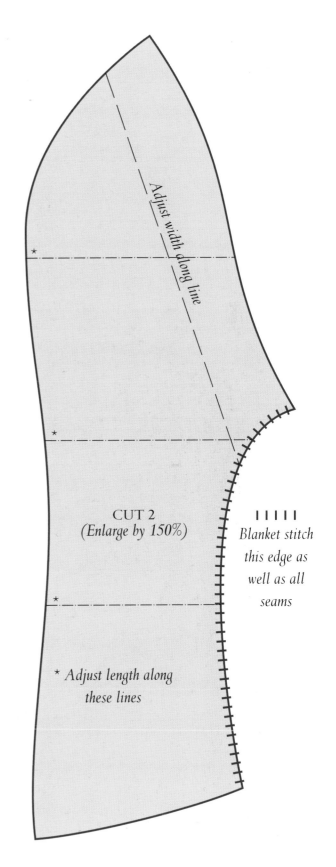

Adjust width along line

★

CUT 2
(Enlarge by 150%)

★

★

★ *Adjust length along these lines*

| | | | |

Blanket stitch this edge as well as all seams

daisy barrette

PAGE 74

CUT 2
(Enlarge by 150%)

love-heart pin

PAGE 78

CUT 2
(Actual size)

earflap hat

PAGE 86

CUT 2
(Enlarge by 170%)

Alter width
(head measurement)
along these lines

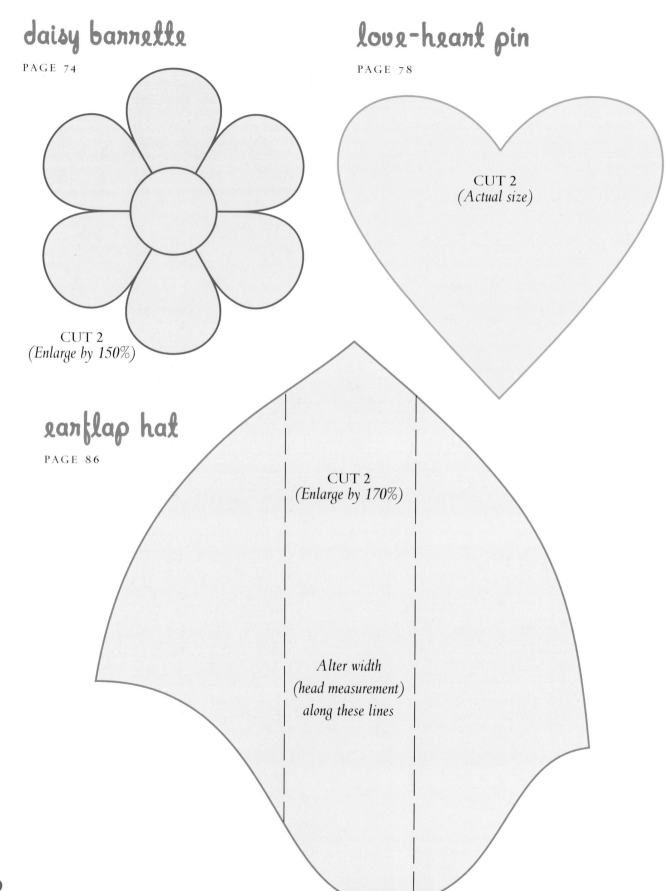

butterfly baby coat

PAGE 94

BACK

CUT 1
(Enlarge by 150%)

Cut on fold

Alter width along this line

CUT 2
(Enlarge by 150%)

CUT 2
(Enlarge by 150%)

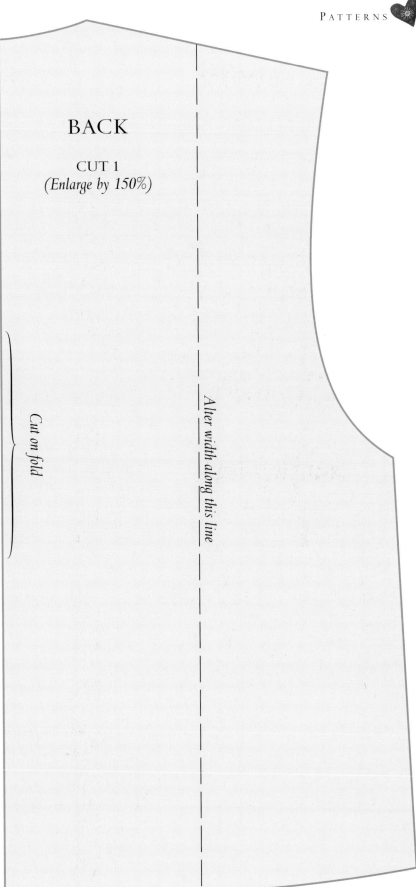

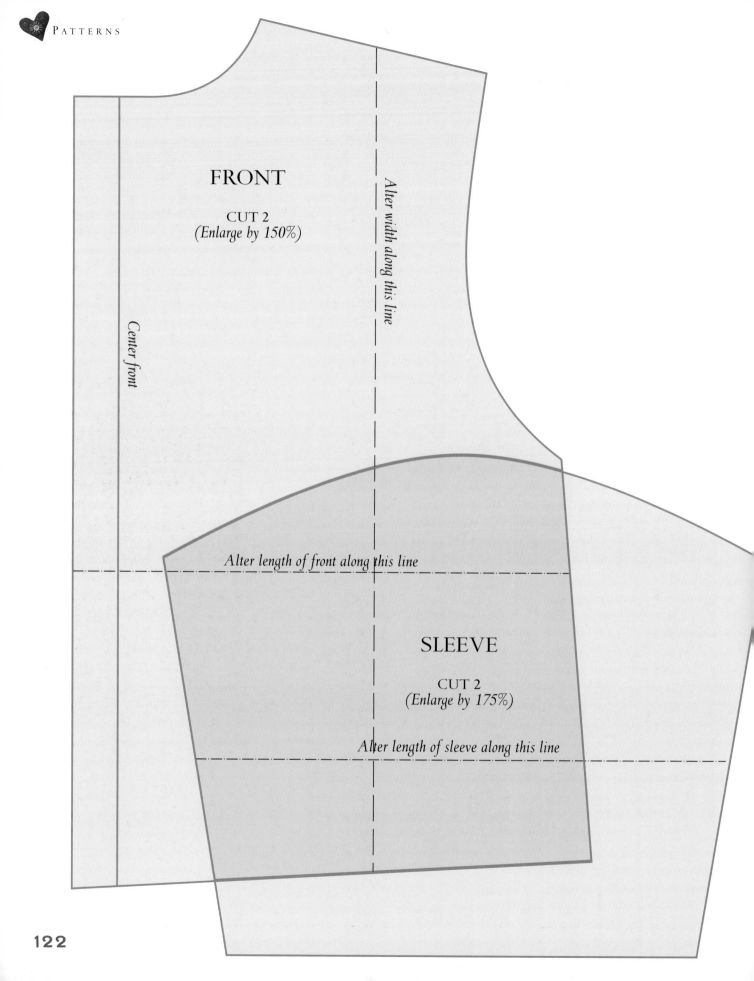

FRONT

CUT 2
(Enlarge by 150%)

Center front

Alter width along this line

Alter length of front along this line

SLEEVE

CUT 2
(Enlarge by 175%)

Alter length of sleeve along this line

cosmic baby blanket

PAGE 100

A

7 x 9 in. (18 x 23 cm)

B

7 x 21 in. (18 x 53 cm)

C

19 x 19 in. (48 x 48 cm)

D

19 x 11 in. (48 x 28 cm)

E

9 x 29 in. (23 x 73 cm)

bunny slippers

PAGE 108

 *Blanket stitch these edges as well as all seams*

BACK SECTION

CUT 4
(Enlarge by 160%)

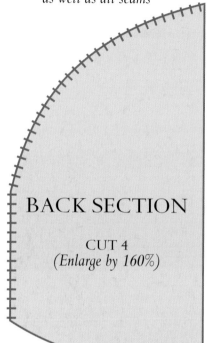

FRONT SECTION

CUT 2
(Enlarge by 160%)

Center front

Adjust width along this line

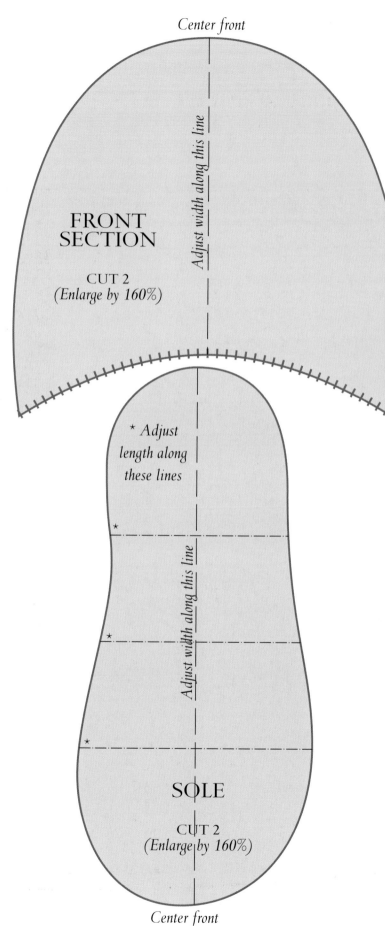

★ *Adjust length along these lines*

Adjust width along this line

SOLE

CUT 2
(Enlarge by 160%)

Center front

EARS

CUT 8
(Enlarge by 160%)

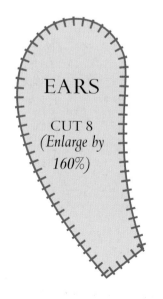

backpack with bird

PAGE 112

FRONT AND BACK

CUT 2
(Enlarge by 160%)

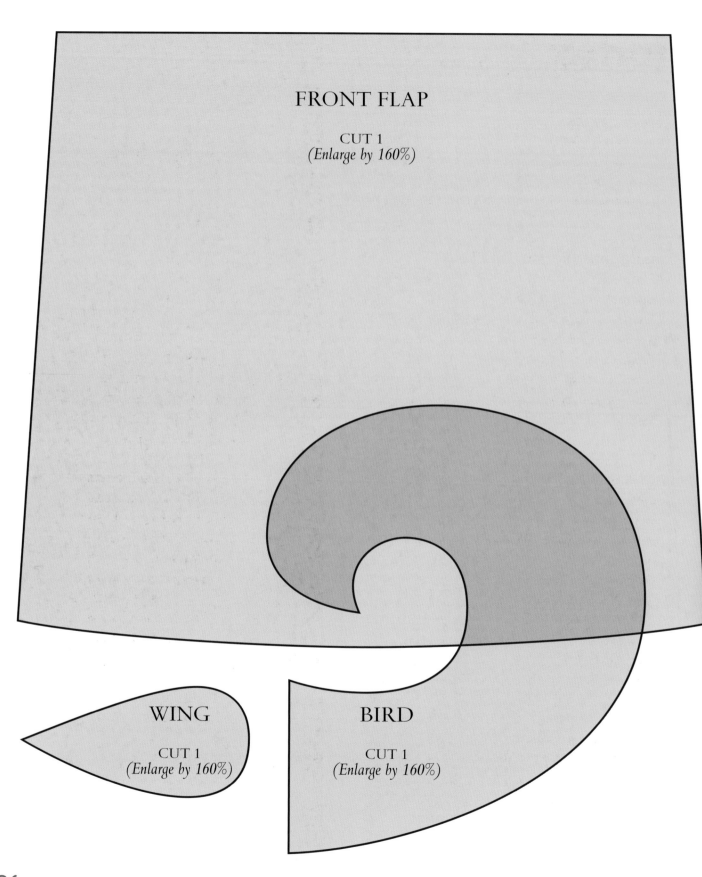

FRONT FLAP

CUT 1
(Enlarge by 160%)

WING

CUT 1
(Enlarge by 160%)

BIRD

CUT 1
(Enlarge by 160%)

index

A

accessories 70–72, *70–73*, 74–81, *74–81*
appliqué, hand 18–19, *18–19*
    machine 16–17, *16–17*

B

Backpack With Bird 112–115, *112–115*
bags 44–53, *44–53*, 82–85, *83–85*
    children's 112–115, *112–115*
blanket, baby's 100–103, *100–103*
Bubble Bag 82–85, *83–85*
Bubble Scarf 82–83, *82–83*
Bunny Slippers 108–111, *108–111*
Butterfly Baby Coat 94–99, *94–99*

C

Children's Mittens 90–93, *90–93*
children's projects 86–115, *86–115*
coat, baby's 94–99, *94–99*
collage, experimenting with 15, *15*
colors, choosing 15, *15*
Cosmic Baby Blanket 100–103, *100–103*

D

Daisy Barrette 74–75, *74–75*
design tips 15, *15*

E

Earflap Hat 86–89, *86–89*
embroidery, hand 18–19, *18–19*
embroidery, free-motion 17, *17*
    machine 16–17, *16–17*

F

felted knitting 11–14, *11–14*
    caring for 14
felting process 14
Flower Mittens 54–57, *54–57*
Freeform Scarf 68–69, *68–69*

G

Glasses Case 36–39, *36–39*

H

hand knitting 13, *13*
hats 22–31, *22–31*
    children's 86–89, *86–89*
Heartwarming Scarf 104–107, *104–107*

I

iPod Case 62–65, *62–65*

L

Lavender Needle Case 40–43, *40–43*
Love-heart Pin 78–81, *78–81*

M

machine knitting 12, *12*
materials and equipment 10, *10*
Midnight Flower Hat 22–27, *22–27*
mittens 54–57, *54–57*
    children's 90–93, *90–93*

O

Oriental Slippers 58–61, *58–61*

P

patterns 116–126, *116–126*
Pom-pom Hair Band 76–77, *76–77*
purse 32–35, *32–35*

R

readymade felt 11
recycling woolens 13
Rose Accessories 70–72, *70–73*
Russian Hat 28–31, *28–31*

S

Sapphire Scarf 66–67, *66–67*
scarf, machine knitting a 12
scarves 66–69, *66–69*, 82–83, *82–83*
    children's 104–107, *104–107*
scrapbooks, keeping 15, *15*
slippers 58–61, *58–61*
    children's 108–111, *108–111*
Star and Button Purse 32–35, *32–35*
Starburst Handbag 44–49, *44–49*
stitches: back 19, *19*; buttonhole 18, *18*; chain 19, *19*; cross 19, *19*; herringbone 19, *19*; lazy daisy 19, *19*; running 18, *18*; satin 17, *17*; set 17, *17*; stab 18, *18*; star 19, *19*; straight 17, *17*; zigzag 16, *16*

T

test samples 12
Tote Bag 50– 53, *50–53*

Y

yarns 11

suppliers

YARN SUITABLE FOR
FELTING
Brown Sheep Company
100662 County Road 16
Mitchell, Nebraska 69357
(800)826-9136
www.brownsheep.com

Cascade Yarns
www.cascadeyarns.com

Classic Elite Yarns
122 Western Avenue
Lowell, MA 01851-1434
(978) 453- 2837
www.classiceliteyarns.com

Halcyon Yarn
12 School Street
Bath, ME 04530
(800) 341- 0282
www.halcyonyarn.com

Harrisville Designs
Center Village
P.O. Box 806
Harrisville, New Hampshire 03450
(800) 338-9415
www.harrisville.com

Marr Haven Wool Farm
772 39th Street
Allegan, Michigan 49010-9353
(269) 673 8800
www.marrhaven.com

Morehouse Farm
2 Rock City Road
Milian, NY 12571
(845) 758-3710
www.morehousefarm.com
www.morehousemerino.com

Patternworks
Route 25
P.O. Box 1618
Center Harbor, NY 03226-1618
800-438-5464
www.patternworks.com

HAND AND MACHINE
EMBROIDERY THREADS
The DMC Corporation
South Hackensack Avenue
Port Kearny Bldg. 10F
South Kearny, NJ 07032-4688
(973) 589-0606
www.dmc.com

Lacis
3163 Adeline Street
Berkeley, CA 94703
(510) 843-7178
www.lacis.com

HABERDASHERY, BEADS
AND JEWELRY FINDINGS
BJ Craft Supplies
203 Bickford Road
Tivoli, TX 77990
www.bjcraftsupplies.com

Jo Ann Fabric and Crafts
www.joann.com

M&J Trimming
1008 Sixth Avenue
New York, NY 10018
(212) 204-9595
www.mjtrim.com
Good for bag handles

DEDICATION
To the funniest man in Bristol

ACKNOWLEDGMENTS
My thanks and lots of love to Steve
for his patience and support, not
only during the writing of this book
but always when a deadline looms.

Thanks and love to mum, Betty
Searle, for her expertise and for
teaching me everything she knows.
Also thanks to her and my late
father for always allowing us the
freedom to be creative and follow
our dreams.

Thanks to the wonderful ladies I
have met through leading
workshops and giving talks over the
years. Your encouragement to write
this book along with your inspiration
and tips have always been very much
appreciated.

My thanks go to Zara Browning,
who has knitted for me for many
years, including all the felt that has
been included in this book.

Thank you to Janet Ravenscroft for
her great enthusiasm, support, and
guidance throughout the production
of this book. Also thanks to Shona
Wood for her wonderful
photographs and yummy lunches.
Without them this book would
never have happened.

Thanks to my lovely nieces Ines,
Mara, Florie, and Amber, and my
nephew Thor—they are the
inspiration for many of the projects
in the children's section.

Copy-edited by Michelle Pickering
Designed by Elizabeth Healey
Photographs by Shona Wood
Templates by Stephen Dew